All's Well That Ends Swell

All-New Audition Monologues With Alternate Endings

by Jason Milligan

A SAMUEL FRENCH ACTING EDITION

SAMUEL FRENCH

FOUNDED 1830

NEW YORK HOLLYWOOD LONDON TORONTO

SAMUELFRENCH.COM

ISBN 978-0-573-69731-9   Printed in U.S.A.   #29172

IMPORTANT BILLING AND CREDIT
REQUIREMENTS

All producers of *ALL'S WELL THAT ENDS SWELL* *must* give credit to the Author of the Play in all programs distributed in connection with performances of the Play, and in all instances in which the title of the Play appears for the purposes of advertising, publicizing or otherwise exploiting the Play and/or a production. The name of the Author *must* appear on a separate line on which no other name appears, immediately following the title and *must* appear in size of type not less than fifty percent of the size of the title type.

FOREWORD

For years, I've toyed with the notion of creating a monologue book that featured alternate endings for each piece – but for some reason, it never came to fruition. Then, one day, I realized that audition monologues should be as individual and as *customizable* as possible – and that the way to achieve the greatest customization would be to allow the actor to actually *participate* in the creation of his or her own monologue.

That's why, in this collection, I've written 50 new audition monologues, each of which comes with two possible endings – for a total of 100 monologues. But I also give the reader an opportunity, if he/she so desires, to create his/her *own* ending. In this way, the collection offers limitless possibilities for variety, spontenaeity and individuality. Please refer to the appendix at the back of the book for specific instructions on how to craft your own conclusions.

Enjoy the pieces, choose your favorite ending...or finish them however you like! Remember, "All's Well That Ends Swell!"

– Jason Milligan
Fall 2009

TABLE OF CONTENTS

For Violet...the "swellest" ending of all!

DOGLESS MARRIAGE

HE. I did not kill the dog! *(pause)* On purpose. No, no, Sheila, listen to me – it was only a *shove*! A mild – well, okay, a *hefty* – shove. I know. I know I had my shoe on, what difference does *that* make? No! No, it wasn't a kick. A kick would be like – *(demonstrates:)* – *that*. It was more like *(demonstrates:)* – *this*. A *nudge* out of the way. I mean put yourself in my shoes. Well, not *shoes*, maybe, but…I mean, I walk in here and he's, he's peeing in my $400 loafers! From Italy! What would **you** have done? Ah, scratch that – I know what you would have done. You'd have picked him up and cooed at him and kissed him on his little doggie lips! But any other person – any *normal* person – would be incensed! Any *reasonable* person would lash out in frustration! I mean, Sheila, COME ON! How was I to know you'd left the window open? How was I to know my gentle tap would send him flying out the –? *(reacts)* What? That's ridiculous! No…no, the dog is *not* an extension of you! You're *you* and the dog is – *was* – the dog. *(beat)* Of *course* I can say his name. *(face scrunches up with distaste) Reginald.* All right? There. I said it. *(pause)* Look…I know you think that this was some subversive ploy on my part. To do away with him…but I promise you, it wasn't. It was just an honest reaction. I saw my Italian loafers and the stream of pee and the dog and – boom! I simply reacted. I mean, c'mon! That was the sixth pair of loafers this month! Not to mention the time when he hiked his leg over my laptop…or my coffee…and God knows how many pairs of my trousers have been saturated with his urine. Look, Sheila… you know I love you. When I took those vows, I meant them. I love you so much, I was even willing to take… Reginald…as part of the bargain. But he just went too far.

ENDING 1

He would wake me up six, seven times a night. He chewed up every material possession I valued. He even watched us when we had sex! It was like you came into the marriage with a child. An evil child. A bad seed. He was doing everything he could to keep us apart! *(rolls eyes)* C'mon, Sheila, even you have to admit, me waking up in the middle of the night to find him trying to gnaw off my wiener…he was pure evil! Just…give me a chance. Let's try a dogless marriage. You owe me at least that much…don't you?

ENDING 2

I will buy you a new dog, Sheila…a sweet dog…the kind of dog who will give us a tiny smidgeon of privacy! Don't we deserve at least a sliver of privacy?! We're newlyweds, for crying out loud! There must be a dog out there, somewhere, who can respect that. Can we try to find *that* dog? If you're willing to find him, then I'm willing to give it a chance. What do you say?

ENDING 3

_____

_____

_____

_____

_____

_____

_____

_____

THE ULTIMATUM

SHE. What? You – *what*??! You want me to *house-sit* for you?!
Is that what this is all about? Good God, Erwin! I
thought you were going to *propose* to me! What do you
mean, "why?" Because! You tell me to get all dressed
up, you take me out to this nice restaurant...candle-
light...soft music...prices that are through the roof...
why *else* would you take a woman to a place like this? To
propose! Well, I'm sorry if *you're* not ready to get married, but I am. I have waited...and waited...and I'm
through waiting! In fact, I'm so through that I'm ready
to issue an ultimatum: marry me, or I won't house-sit!
There! I've said it! Your goldfish will die, your plants
will wither and your cat will pee all over the carpet
because there'll be nobody there to take care of them!
What? Yes, I'm *totally* serious! You don't believe me?
Why? What is it about you? Why does the whole idea of
marriage totally *elude* you so thoroughly? It's not like
you're an idiot! *(realizes:)* Or maybe you *are* an idiot
and I simply refuse to see it... *(then, back to the topic
at hand:)* Either way, I'm making my wants and needs
known, once and for all! *(snapping at a waiter:)* NO!
We're NOT ready to order yet! *(back to Erwin:)* You
once said that you and I were a "we." Yes, you did. You
did. Last Fourth of July, when we were watching the
fireworks, you said, "I'm so glad we have each other."
What exactly did you mean by that? To house-sit for
one another? Don't take me for granted, Erwin. You
may think that I'm something you never have to really
deal with, like a zit that'll just go away all by itself, but
you'd better face reality. Because I could get snapped-
up like...*(snaps fingers)* ...that!

ENDING 1

You don't believe me? *(calls off:)* Oh, waiter? Waiter! *(to an unseen waiter:)* Hi…*(reads name tag:)* Federico. I'd like another glass of ginger-ale and would you marry me? No, I'm not kidding. I'm proving a point! *(pause)* Well, I'll give you my number, then, and you can let me know. *(back to Erwin:)* You see, Erwin? I may not be on the market forever! This could be your last chance. So take a stand now, or lose me forever…to Federico!

ENDING 2

Don't laugh at me! Of course I could! You have no idea who's harboring romantic thoughts of me. I have my high school reunion coming up next month, and there's bound to be some guy there who pined after me all through high school and he's just waiting for me to show up and he'll sweep me up in his arms and…oh, what's the use? I'll house-sit for you, Erwin. Now get the waiter over here and let's order. I suddenly have a monster of a headache.

ENDING 3

_____

_____

_____

_____

_____

_____

_____

_____

_____

LIFE RAGE

HE. Bob, I'm sorry, but this whole "arrangement" isn't working out. Bob? Bob! For cryin' out loud! Will you take those headphones off and listen? I'm talking to you! About *what*? About this whole *carpooling* thing! I can't take it anymore! Because! You are annoying, Bob. Yes. Annoying! To the "nth" degree! "Like what?" Like everything! Everything about you! Don't you ever wonder why I always drive with the window down? In the dead of winter? Because your breath is like a toxic waste dump! And no matter what you wear, it smells stale and disgusting. My clothes have taken on your foul odor! And my beautiful new car...look at it! It's a mess! You sit there, clipping those waxy yellow toe-nails and sending your clippings ricocheting off the dashboard...and to top all that off, you seem to have an endless supply of gas! And even all *that* might be bearable if this were a ten-minute commute, but it's an hour and a half! Each way! *Every day!* Do you realize how many hours of irritation that adds up to? 5,000 hours a year! You're shortening my life, Bob, I can feel it – the stress that you're causing me is taking years off my life! I've lost twenty pounds since you started riding with me... I can't sleep at night...and I've been rendered impotent! Of *course* it's your fault! Because! You disgust me! You irritate me! You infuriate me! I never had road rage until I took you on as a carpool buddy and now I have LIFE RAGE! I constantly want to whack, run over or smash everything and everybody I see – because of you! You make every weekday start off miserably and every weekday *end* miserably! And who can enjoy the weekend, dreading Monday the whole time. I can't do this anymore, Bob. My only solace is my vacation…two weeks a year away from you. And most of that time is spent either in therapy, fumigating the car or dry cleaning all my clothes!

ENDING 1

You have to get out and walk, Bob. Now. I mean it. If I keep you in the car two more minutes, I will lose it and kill you. Along with anybody else in my path. That is how livid I am inside. I may be covering it up, I may be holding it in, but the lid is barely on. This volcano is going to blow any second…and you don't want to be in that passenger seat when it does. Now, get out, Bob. I mean it. It's for your own good.

ENDING 2

Look, Bob. I'll find someone else to drive you to work. Who? I don't know yet! Maybe Renaldo, in grounds services. He could pick you up in his gardening truck. And of course, there's always the bus. *(beat)* I don't care how long it takes, the point is, you no longer have a seat in this car anymore. I'll wrench it out and throw it on the side of the road if I have to…but the point is: your seat is gone. Now, Bob. Are you hearing me? Bob? Bob! Are you *asleep*?!

ENDING 3

_____
_____
_____
_____
_____
_____
_____
_____

WALKING COMPLAINT

SHE. It's not "just a migraine!" I'm practically dying here, can't you see that? It's like I have a tiny jackhammer in the inside of my skull, this continuous pounding that begins the moment you walk into the room and never lets up until you *leave*! Oh, I wish you could feel it – the pain I endure, all because of the fact that you exist! Goodness gracious, Arthur. If only for five minutes you had to endure half of what I've had to suffer, all because of you, you selfish, stupid man! *(beat)* You are! You think only about yourself and your own hysterics. Always going on and on about what "problems" you have and what a "victim" you are…hours and hours of "woe is me"…it's enough to make me choke on my own bile! *(reacts with shock:)* I am *not* a Drama Queen! How dare you call me that! You'd think I was the one who complained all the time! It's *you* who complains, Arthur! You who whines and moans about his, oh, his Acid Reflux and that stupid ulcer of yours…well, then drink some Maalox and stop complaining! Why couldn't I have a *real* man? A stalwart man! Instead I've got a Walking Complaint! It's not like you've had to go through what I've gone through…and yet you have the nerve to come in here and stand there in the doorway, bitching about being asked to stand out there in the cold for a few minutes to hail me a cab? All right, *twenty* minutes! Put a coat on, then, Arthur – for goodness sakes! Or a sweater! But don't come in here whining about what a victim you are! There's only room enough for one victim in this townhouse and it's *me*! Do you understand?

ENDING 1

Either you show some compassion to me, or you're out on your rear end! And don't think I won't throw you out! I've done it before! That time you told me you didn't find me attractive anymore – did you ever wonder why those thugs pummeled you in that alley? I *arranged* it! So don't mess with me, Arthur, unless you're ready to fight back! You either love me – and do what I tell you – or it's the street for you! Have I made myself clear? Now. Get out of here before my migraine escalates. I need to rest.

ENDING 2

Mother was right, Arthur. She told me that you'd make me play second fiddle to you. I said, no, he'll put me first forever and ever. What a fool I was. You only care about yourself and your own selfish self interests – *(winces:)* Ooh! My head! Shut up, Arthur! Either look me in the eyes and tell me that I mean everything to you – like you mean it – or get out of here! *(softens:)* Thank you, darling...you *do* love me!

ENDING 3

_____
_____
_____
_____
_____
_____
_____
_____

ANOTHER DAY IN BUZZARD CREEK

HE. You try slopping the hogs and see how "joyful" you are, Maybelle! Honestly. You'd think you had grown up in some kinda rich family, the way you act. Puttin' on airs, all the time. You grew up on your pappy's farm, same as me. You dropped outta school in sixth grade, same as me. Oh. Sorry. Seventh. You really lasted, didn't you? You worked at the Arby's for a few years and now you're better than me? You can't get out there and slop the hogs and feed the chickens? You got to sit in here with your feet up and your hair wrapped in tinfoil and watch that durn TV and paint your nails and judge everybody else. That's what you're doin', Maybelle. Judgin' all the rest of us. *(for example:)* You told the Reverend Fudge that his *teeth* needed fixin'. And maybe they do, but you don't say things like that to the preacher. In front of other people! And you told Billy Ray Wilkins that he needed to wear shoes to church! Since when do mountain folk wear shoes to church, Maybelle? And speakin' of shoes, you got way too many pairs. It ain't fittin' for one person to own more'n two pairs of shoes and you got seven! Seven pairs of shoes! For what, I ask you? Any normal human bean just needs two pairs of shoes – boots for workin' and Sunday shoes for churchin'. What are all them high heels for? Fancy dance balls? I don't recollect seein' any fancy dance balls in Buzzard Creek! This has got to stop, Maybelle. You puttin' yourself above everybody else. And even me, your own husband! Why, when we took our vows, you was so happy to get outta the Arby's and start a life with me…nowadays you just seem angry all the time.

ENDING 1

You got to get over it, Maybelle! Stop whinin' and start sloppin'! Them hogs can't feed themselves and I can't keep doin' all the work around here! When you took them vows, you said you'd stand by me, no matter what! Well, last time I looked, I was doin' all the standin' alone! Now get on up outta that chair and – high heels or no – come out and help me milk the cow!

ENDING 2

What happened, Maybelle? How could you change in so short a time? Is it them TV shows puttin' ideas in your head? I thought I knew what was in your head, 'fore we married. Now I reckon I don't know nothin'. I'm hopin' you'll still want to make a go of things with me...Lord knows I can't do it alone. But you got to meet me halfway. What do you say, Maybelle? Do we still got us a chance?

ENDING 3

_____
_____
_____
_____
_____
_____
_____
_____

BUSY PEOPLE

SHE. Explain this to me, Glum…in terms I can understand. How could you set another boy's *hair* on fire? *(beat)* No, no, I *understand* that you used matches. What I mean is, *why?* Why on earth would you ever think to do something like that in the first place? It's egregious! Well, you *should* know what that means by now. All the money we spend to send you to that fancy boarding school…and how do you pay us back? By igniting another child's hair! A disabled child, no less – oh, can you even begin to imagine how big the lawsuit will be? My nerves just frazzle thinking about it! And, worst of all – expelled! Yes, expelled from the Simon T. Mankowski Academy for Young Men. You just wait 'til your father gets home. Yes. Cairo. And I leave for Morocco on Tuesday. Could you have picked a more inconvenient moment to torch another child? You could have waited a few weeks, until we were both on the same continent at least! But no – you've got to choose this moment to act out! We are busy people, Glum! We don't have time to put out your fires – oh – bad choice of words, that. I mean, mop up your messes. That's why we sent you to boarding school in the first place! So that responsible people could look after you. Watch over you. Shape you into a fine young man. Not a fiendish little pyromaniac! Why, it's not *our* fault we don't have more time to spend with you! We are successful, Glum! Your father and I are successful people! Not everyone is as sought after as we are, you should be proud of that!

ENDING 1

All right, Glum. Listen to me...I need a little R&R before my voyage to Morocco. I cannot leave the country with my nerves on edge. So I'll have your Great Uncle Waldo come and stay with you. Just promise me you won't set him on fire! With all the alcohol he consumes, he's bound to be extremely flammable!

ENDING 2

I know we haven't been exactly...well...available, at all times...but we've always tried to set you up in the best boarding schools, haven't we? The finest summer camps, the highest-rated after-school programs! Why, you had the most expensive day care in Twin Oaks! We are your parents. It's our job to hire the best care for you. You understand, don't you? Don't you? *(alarmed:)* Glum? Glum! *Put down those matches this instant!!*

ENDING 3

_____

_____

_____

_____

_____

_____

_____

_____

SIDE EFFECTS

HE. Ow! My tooth! I chipped my tooth! *(beat)* What do you mean, on *what?* On those *biscuits* of yours! *(fiddling with a front tooth:)* Is it cracked? I think it's cracked. Well, I just hope Dr. Berg can take me. Maybe he can put a cap on it, or…I dunno. *(sighs)* I *swear!* This is just another in a long line of side effects, Velma. Yes, side effects. Like with medication? Only these seem to come from being engaged to *you! (for example:)* Every time *you* hail a cab, the driver gets lost or runs over a cat – I know it was just an accident, but every time *I* hail one, we get where we're going just fine! Without any casualties! Not to mention the Elevator Thing. Whenever you push the button, the elevator gets stuck between floors or the alarm goes off or something horrific happens. And or course, there's all of *my* injuries! No, it hasn't gotten "better." You accidentally hit, kick or whack me once a day, minimum! Whenever you're getting into a car, or walking through a door or opening a cabinet – smack! I get it in the head, gut or groin. Perhaps you're just clumsy. But that's impossible, because usually you are the most graceful person I've ever seen! Maybe it's just when you're around *me*! *(sighs:)* I guess I don't know what it is, Velma. I fell in love with you because you made my heart skip a beat…but now I'm afraid you're going to make it stop beating altogether. No! No, this is not about the ladder. *(beat)* Well, maybe it is. Maybe it *is* about the ladder. I mean, c'mon. When you see a guy – your fiancée, no less – on the roof of the house and there's a ladder out there…okay, so you didn't see it and knocked it over by accident…but why wouldn't you put it back up again? Who *wouldn't* put the ladder back? Anybody would put the ladder back! Except for you, Velma.

ENDING 1

Maybe it's time we...you know. Took a break. From each other. Maybe we suspend the engagement. No, no – I didn't say "cancel," all right? I said "suspend." No, this is not about me getting cold feet. But I don't want to wind up cold all over. And I'm just afraid...that if we don't pause and assess our situation...that you're going to – accidentally – do me in!

ENDING 2

I don't know what it is...but no matter how much you abuse me, I can't stay away. You're like this living, breathing bug zapper and I'm the bug, drawn to the light. I don't know what the light holds for me... maybe my doom...but I can't fly away. You completely captivate me, Velma. And I suppose that's worth a few bruised ribs and broken bones. So what d'ya say we head over to Dr. Berg's and see if he can fix my tooth? But if you don't mind...*I'll* hail the cab!

ENDING 3

_____

_____

_____

_____

_____

_____

_____

_____

EVERY MOMENT

SHE. Do you remember when we were kids? Summer seemed to last...forever. Endless day after endless day, all of them filled with beautiful, mundane pursuits like hunting for seashells...or playing hide and seek out in the woods...swimming in the lake...those three months of summer seemed like they would never end. *(beat)* What happened, Alan? Time just began to, I dunno, *accelerate* somehow. Days fly past in what seems like seconds, and now, summer seems to flash past us in the blink of an eye. Years go by like that – *(snaps fingers)* – and the innocence that was such an indelible part of those childhood summers...is gone. *(beat)* As you can imagine, the days don't rush by quite as quickly for me as they used to. I suppose a lot of that has to do with being shut up in here and confined to a bed. Now, don't get me wrong. I'm not feeling sorry for myself. It's just, all those precious seconds...minutes...hours...that used to whoosh by like a speeding train...well, I try to use them now. Every one of them. No more wasted time watching game shows or listening to the radio or playing solitaire. Every moment that I have now, I use it. I think...I plan...and I hope... that I'll still have a tomorrow...and a next week...and maybe even a next year. And if things work out and I *do* have some more time, I've decided that I want to share that time with you.

ENDING 1

I know, I know. You're probably looking at me and thinking, "Good God, what do I want with a broken-down wreck like her?" Well, my body may be shattered from the accident, but my heart is whole...at least it will be, if I can be with you. *(beat)* So what do you say, Alan? All that I can promise is, if you'll have me...we'll make every moment count.

ENDING 2

(beat) I see. Well, who could blame you? Broken down old wreck like me?! I guess when we're young, we feel like we're invincible...like we're super-men – or women. But the world is filled with Kryptonite...and one day, you might find your own Kryptonite and be surprised at how vulnerable you are. I just hope you have somebody there with you when that happens.

ENDING 3

_____

_____

_____

_____

_____

_____

_____

_____

BOY IN THE BOX

HE. I feel like I just got kicked in the head. No, really. Every time you show up, it makes me feel that way. I reckon it's all that you done in the past that's added up over the years. *(beat)* You came here for – what? To wish me a "Happy Birthday?" Well, thanks, Pop. What about some of my other birthdays…do you remember my sixth birthday? Sure ya do. I remember it like it was yesterday. It was the night you made me sleep in a cardboard box. You said, "It's a space ship, Ricky!" It was a refrigerator box that you got from – I dunno. It sure wasn't from a new refrigerator, 'cause you never bought us one of those. Mom went to her grave, wishing – just once – that you'd bought her something nice. Anyway, you cut a hatch in the side of the box with your switchblade. And you told me, "Now, climb in there and whatever you do, don't come out. I'll tell you when you've made it to Mars, but don't come out 'til I tell you." You said if I came out of the box before you said so, I'd be killed by the asteroids. Well, I was a kid, so I believed you. And I laid in that box all night. Fell asleep in there. Found you the next morning with a bunch of empty liquor bottles and some floozy you must've found at the pool hall. And – I will never forget this part – she opened her made-up eyelids, looked at me and said, "Who is that?" And you rolled over and fixed yer bloodshot eyes on me and said, "Damned if I know." And you went back to sleep. *(beat)* And so here we are…all these years later…and you got the balls to show up at my house? On my birthday? What do you need, pop? Money for a drink?

ENDING 1

Well, you won't get no help from me, old man. You got that? That little kid who trusted you, the one you put into that box all those years ago, he ain't never goin' back into it again. You musta figured I'd never grow up and have ideas of my own, did ya? But I do. And I'm strong. I guess I got *you* to thank for that. You're the one who made me strong by treating me like crap all those years. So keep on walking, pop. I ain't gonna be kicked in the head by you no more.

ENDING 2

Well, I'll tell you what. I'll give you twenty bucks. 'Cause I aim to be what *you* never were – decent. But that don't mean I got to love you. You may be my flesh and blood, but I don't got to love you. You can stay the night if you got nowhere else to stay, I won't be the one who turned you out. But you got a lot of provin' to do if you want me to believe you've changed. There may be some trust left in me yet, pop. But you are gonna have to earn it back, one truth at a time.

ENDING 3

_____

_____

_____

_____

_____

_____

_____

_____

STUPID AND POPULAR

SHE. *(wildly offended:)* I can't *believe* you would say something like that to me! Out of the blue! To just yell
it out in public like that?! You should be ashamed,
Harold! *(beat)* No! Once and for all – listen to me –
I am *not* "smart." *(shudders)* Ugh! I feel like you just
poured *sewage* all over me or something. To even *think*
that – to lump me in with all the brainy, nerdy kids
like that! I'm not smart, Harold, all right? I'm *popular*! When are you ever gonna get it through that thick
head of yours? I don't *want* to be smart! I don't want to
be on the Dean's List! I want to get invited to Debbie
Chocodero's party! I want to drink lots of Jell-O shoot-
ers and puke all over her parents' carpet! I want to be
wildly well-known, marry somebody who's got a huge
trust fund one day, jet all over the world and live out
my life shopping at the most expensive stores on the
planet! I don't aspire to solve world hunger or crack
the secret of DNA or whatever it is you think I can
do! I fail tests on *purpose*, all right? *(beat)* What do you
mean, you know? If you know, then you know I don't
want anybody else to know. Know what I mean? *(shakes
her head, sighs)* Oh, it's useless! Listen. You're a Smart
Geek. Okay? I respect that. You know everything there
is to know about math and science and that's great –
but I can't take a risk on you. True, you may grow up
to be Bill Gates and have two hundred billion dollars
or something and I'll be kicking myself…but on the
other hand, you may just turn out to be some poor,
ugly nerd who earns minimum wage sitting in some
awful, disgusting cubicle job someplace. Hey, I'm just
being honest! Right now you have zits all over your
face, you smell like a dog's butt and I would rather

die than kiss you with all those braces on your teeth. *(beat)* It doesn't matter that they come off next month, Harold. You're not hearing me!

ENDING 1

You don't have a *chance* with me! All right? Well, I take that back...you have a one million and seventy-four to one chance. But that's the last time I'm doing a math problem in my head! I don't want to come off as smart anymore – and I don't want you asking me out, all right? I want you to leave me alone and let me be stupid and popular. Now get out of my way, Harold! I've got a trust fund boy to snag!

ENDING 2

Look. I don't want to get your hopes up or anything... but if you can find some way to prove to me that you're going to be financially viable one day – and by "viable" I mean way over-the-top rich – oh, and at least moderately attractive – *then* I will consider letting you call me. But until that time, just stay away from me. It's not personal. I've just got to hedge my bets. Because when we all come back for our tenth anniversary reunion...I want to be at the top of the heap!

ENDING 3

_____
_____
_____
_____
_____
_____
_____
_____

CLAY GOPHERS

HE. I don't know why you always gotta yell at me. I may be a "hillbilly" and I may not know as many big ol' long book words as you, but I still know a lot, Hessie. "Like what?" Well, like…like, I know how to skin a squirrel and cook it in a pot while a blindin' black rain pours down on my head. I'll bet you can't a done that. I could live off seeds and berries for weeks – *months*, if I had to – and I bet you can't a done that. No. No, I'm not sayin' I'm *better'n* you. You can do things I can't do. I know for a fact you'd last a lot longer in a library than me, that's for sure. I wouldn't even know how to find the outhouse. I mean, bathroom. I'd be wanderin' up and down them aisles of books like some lost sheep…and there ain't no sun in them places neither, is there? Still, you don't gotta act like you're better'n me and Ratchet. Him and me's done okay on our own. Fixed this place up nice. Well, maybe not as nice as *your* place in New York City prob'ly is, but for out here in the backwoods, it's mighty nice. 'Member how you used to hate to go out in the rain to get to the outhouse? *(points:)* Well, lookie there. Ratchet and me put a cover up so's you don't get wet no more. *(proudly:)* It's plastic and tin and stretches all the way from the back door to the outhouse! Oh, and Ratchet makes clay gophers and we sell 'em to the tourists that come up the hill. For twenty bucks, some o' them people will even pay you to take 'em out and shoot somethin' for 'em. What would Ratchet shoot in New York City? Huh? You see what I'm sayin'? This is home for Ratchet and me. It's all we've ever known.

ENDING 1

Look, you don't gotta be worried about us. And you don't gotta come back and act like we's helpless and can't live without you. We've lived without you all these years. Ever since Pop died. No reason we can't keep doin' just fine on our own. I know what you want. You wanna bring us two hillbillies back to New York and poof us up to look and act and talk like you. Well, it ain't gonna happen, Hessie. Not while I'm around. You can take your fancy suitcase and head on back to the big pineapple. Ratchet and me is sayin' put.

ENDING 2

Y'know…you could come back, if'n you wanted to. Ratchet and me kept your room just like Maw had it. Yer stuffed animals. We could get you a new pet rat. There's plenty of rats out there in the woods. *(beat)* Oh. Well 'course not. Once you've tasted the big pineapple, why would you wanna come back here? But…all the same, we'll still keep your room for ya. In case you change your mind. This'll always be yer home, Hessie. Whether you like it or not.

ENDING 3

_____

_____

_____

_____

_____

_____

_____

_____

EMOTIONAL BAROMETER

SHE. *(hyperventilating in shock:)* Oh, my God! I am just now, at this very moment, having a major realization – and it's not good. Not good at all. *(fights to catch her breath.)* You don't *know* me! You don't! I just asked you, "Do you know what would be really romantic right now?" And you said, "Yes, hot cider by the fireplace in that little café over there." But that wasn't what I was thinking at *all*! I was thinking, "lap blankets and a carriage ride through Central Park in the freezing rain." We had *two different romantic images*, Richard! Don't you see? That means we're polar opposites! We're Venus and Mars! *(beat)* No. No, I completely disagree. A romantic idea like that is more than just a mental image – it's a *barometer*, Richard. An emotional barometer. And ours are completely out of sync! We're miles apart! Miles! If we were meant to be together – truly *meant*, by whatever cosmic forces – we would have had the exact same mental image! *(beat)* What? How do I know? Oh, I just know. Ever since I was a little girl, I knew, deep in my veins, that when I met the right man, the one I was going to marry…that we would have the same thoughts, the same ideas, the same wishes, the same dreams – What? No! It would not make you a "girl" if you had the exact same dreams as me. I'm not talking about *all* of your dreams, just the ones that we share! Ours! Everything we think, say and do should be in sync. Matching. Identical. But that's not how it us with us. I see that now! We don't even order the same food when we go out to eat. Last night, I got the manicotti and you got… *(gulp!)* …scallops!

ENDING 1

Well…at least I know the truth now, don't I? I can stop wasting my future, hoping that one day, we'll see eye to eye. It's amazing how blind you can be when you're in love, isn't it? I mean, all this time I thought we had the same wants, the same wishes, the same…oh, what's the word? *(brightens:)* Yes! *Desires!* You said exactly what I was thinking! You – *(realizes:)* Well, maybe there *is* hope for us, Richard. Maybe we *do* see eye-to-eye after all!

ENDING 2

I can't marry a man who eats scallops! I don't like scallops! I don't even know exactly what scallops *are!* What are they, anyway? Oh, never mind! That's not the point! I know your friends think I'm completely irrational, but my instincts have always ruled my choices. And my instincts are telling me to back off and find someone else. There has to be someone out there for me who thinks exactly like I do. *(pause)* Very funny. Well, maybe I *will* try the "mental ward." Ha, ha. But now hear this: we are through. And I mean it!

ENDING 3

_____

_____

_____

_____

_____

_____

_____

_____

DEAD QUIET

HE. I think I just killed my landlord. I'm not kidding. He was yelling about how there was no way he was gonna fix that leak in the roof and it was, like, the millionth time he'd called me a "loser." And…I dunno…something snapped. I threw a chicken at him. That's right, one of the – oh, I'm sorry. *Hen*. One of the hens. I forgot, we only raise hens. For their eggs. Anyway, he kept saying that all the neighbors were complaining about the noise. Now, I ask you…how much noise does a chick – *(corrects himself)* – *hen* – really make? A little bok-bok-bokking now and then? They're dead quiet otherwise. I told him, I said, well, if the roof didn't leak on their little heads, they probably wouldn't make so much noise! And then – get this – he had the nerve to complain about the cows! I told him, I said, doesn't he get to enjoy the fresh milk every other Tuesday? But noooo, he said that the neighbors – and I'm sure it's *those* people *(points up)* – upstairs – he said they were tired of the "mooing." I'll give 'em some mooing… *(Makes loud cow noises:)* Moooo! Mooooo! *(then, back to the topic at hand:)* I can't believe it! Everything was going so good for us and he has the nerve to say that the master bedroom suite is all of a sudden "not the right place" to keep cattle. Oh, and then – *then* he gets started on us using the bathtub for a pig trough – and, well, something in me just snapped! I looked down and there was one of the chi – *hens*. Eunice, I think. Anyway, I just plucked her up and threw her at him! She made this loud screeching sound – I've never heard a hen do that – and boom, down he went like a load of bricks. It was like bowling for landlords! Only, I was using a hen instead of a bowling ball and there was only one pin: the landlord.

ENDING 1

Who? Eunice? Oh, she's okay. A little "hen shock," but I think she'll be all right. The landlord, on the other hand, totally freaked out! He tried to get up and run but he slipped and fell down the stairs – all three flights! He's out in the hen house right now, buried under some straw. I just need to know: is it *my* fault that he's dead? Or the hen's? I really hope you'll say the hens. 'Cause I don't want to be thought of as a murderer.

ENDING 2

Well, he fell. Out the window. And somebody called the police and...well, what am I supposed to do now? The ranch is gonna find out that we stole all these animals...and I hate to say it, but...I think I'm going to have to frame *you*, Harriet. Well, a couple of the neighbors heard you threaten the landlord last month and, well...I think you fit the hen-throwing profile more than I do.

ENDING 3

_____
_____
_____
_____
_____
_____
_____
_____

BACK SIDE OF HELL

SHE. What you's seein' ain't the normal – *(yells at an unseen child:)* Get down off the TV, Wiley! *(back to the conversation:)* Y'see, this ain't what it's usually like around here. *(calls off:)* Rufus! Let go of the porcupine! You'll jab your *other* eye out! *(back to conversation:)* Oh, no. I ain't runnin' no day care. No sir! These kids is from my *sister's* day care. *(calls off:)* Wynona, do not put your finger in that light socket! *(weary:)* Oh, my lord…I dunno how she does it. My sister, I mean. She must just drug 'em all up and wait for the day to end – *(catches herself:)* I don't mean that in a literalistic way. I just meant it in a "so to speak" kinda way. See, my sister, she's got a way with kids. Even Nelmo there. *(yells off:)* Nelmo! Don't eat that roach chalk! Filbee, take that chalk away from him right this instant! But – no! Don't *draw* with it! *(back to conversation:)* They's a lively bunch, ain't they? Okay, now, I know what you're thinkin'. That it ain't right to keep 'em all cooped up in a trailer like this. Well, we don't stay in here all day. We walk. To the park. Across the highway and over the railroad tracks and to the park. They love tip-toein' through all that broken glass. They love stoppin' by the dump to look for treasures. That ol' sayin' is true: one person's crap is another person's gold. Or however it goes. They find all kinds of treasures at the dump. Pet rats, too! Do you wanna see our pet rats? Don't worry, we keep 'em in the shower, with the glass doors closed and some duct tape to keep the doors shut tight. The kids just love tossin' spoilt meat over the top and listenin' to 'em squeal, it's like music when you – *(reacts:)* Well, you could quit wrinklin' up your face like you just set foot in the back side of hell, mister! I am *tryin'* to be hospitable! Speakin' of which, would you like some

Kool-Aid? *(beat)* Well, maybe that's all for the best, I think Wynona mighta peed in it anyway.

ENDING 1

Listen, I don't know who called the police, but it couldn't have been one o' my neighbors, 'cause these kids ain't even here every day and – *(reacts:)* No! No! I swear to you, they ain't *mine* – it's my sister, looks after 'em! If you gotta punish anybody, punish her! Not *me*! *(beat)* Hold on, now...do we *really* need handcuffs? *(beat)* All right. I'll go with ya. But you better make sure somebody comes by to feed the rats...or there's gonna be trouble.

ENDING 2

Look, if you'd just talk to my sister – *(pause)* Oh. Well... how'd you find that she died? All right. Look. Everybody's got to eat, right? So I'll tell you what...I'll give you half of what I take in here. That's $100 a day. I'll give it to you if you back off and find somebody else to pick on. It's not like there's a shortage of crazy people 'round here – it's a trailer park for cryin' out loud! Now, don't answer yet – just take a load off, sit down... and think it over. I'll make up a fresh batch of Kool-Aid for ya...some that hasn't been peed in yet!

ENDING 3

_____
_____
_____
_____
_____
_____
_____
_____

HOLLOW PROMISES

HE. Give me one reason. Give me one good reason why I shouldn't spit in your face. *(fighting back emotions:)* Eighteen months, Natalie! Eighteen months I waited for you! What was I thinking? "Great experience for her. College in Europe." What an idiot! I sat here and *waited* for you! Do you have any idea how hard that was? I thought it might have been just as hard for you, too…but apparently not. Apparently, you *liked* your freedom. You liked being around a lot of other guys, guys who were more educated than me, guys who knew how to talk foreign to you and who had money to buy you things…is that what it was? I was *faithful*, Natalie! I never even *looked* at another girl. I worked at that hell-hole of a garage and I waited. Looking at that calendar every single morning and wishing the days would pass faster. It seemed so far away but I kept telling myself, "You can make it." So I buckled down, dove in and worked. I worked nights. I worked weekends – *anything* to make the time go by. I planned out how I'd meet you at the airport. How I'd throw my arms around you and give you that ring…how your eyes would light up when you saw it…how incredible it would be to see you again after all this time…and how amazing it would feel to hold you again…to remember what your hair smelled like, after living away for so long… but you don't have the time of day for me anymore, do you? I stood there on the tarmac with a friggin' ring box in my hand, waiting – and you had already gone! That jerk's limo picked you up! Did you even see me standing there? Or was it *funny* to you, that old Jeremy was just standing there like a total loser? I'll bet you laughed at me! You and that jerk both! Well, no more, Natalie. I have taken abuse from you and everybody else in this town long enough. From now on, it's gonna be what I want. Or nothing at all.

ENDING 1

So here's what you're gonna do: you're gonna go out there and you're gonna get in my car and we're driving to Vegas. First wedding chapel we come to, we're tying the knot, once and for all. You don't like it – well, too bad. You should've thought of that before you made all those hollow promises to me. *(beat:)* Look at me, Natalie. I mean it. I won't take "no" for an answer.

ENDING 2

Call him, Natalie. I'm serious. I know there's another guy, and I want to meet him. Face to face. I want to see exactly who's stolen you from me. I wanna feel what it's like to beat the living crap out of him. And then I wanna know what it's like to walk away. From both of you. Do you even comprehend what I'm telling you? I handed my heart over to you...and you stomped all over it. But I swear, *nobody* will ever do that to me again.

ENDING 3

_____
_____
_____
_____
_____
_____
_____
_____

WALKING LANDFILL

SHE. *(completely aggravated:)* Can't you even bother to *flush*?!
Good grief, René, I can't believe it! You are a one-man
walking landfill! Mounds of refuse seem to just ema-
nate from you, wherever you go…you deposit trash in
every corner of the house…you emit the foulest odors
that have ever drifted up into human nostrils…oh,
and, to top it all off, you can't be "bothered" to flush
the toilet! *(reacts to something he's said:)* What? *(in a
mock French accent:)* "You didn't notice?" I can't believe
it! There is a turd in there the size of Spain – oh, all
right, *France*, then. – and you "didn't notice?" Well,
did you "notice" that your soiled underwear is strewn
across on my dining room table? Did you "notice" that
you've left your dirty dishes out for nine days straight
and let me clean them up? No. No, don't play that "Je
ne parle Anglais" card with me! You know a lot more
than you pretend to know. How? Because I lied to you,
René! Yes! I told you that I didn't speak any French at
all, but in reality, I've been going to night school! Yes!
Beginning French. I've impressed my teacher, Henri.
He says I'm a natural – and I'm picking up *francais* at
an amazing rate! Which means, now I understand a
lot of what you're saying and believe me, I don't have
to know a lot of French to know that it's complete and
total b.s.! *(reacts:)* No! It is not a "French custom" to
leave the toilet un-flushed! Because! I asked my *French
Teacher*!!

ENDING 1

(beat) Look…when I agreed to have you as an exchange student, that did not include an "exchange" of waste products! But you have consistently taken advantage of me and laughed about it – *laughed*! Well, get in there and pack your bag – if you can find it amongst all the crap! I'm dead serious! You've left your last mess, monsieur! I'm cleaning up, once and for all!

ENDING 2

(beat) Look…I know there's been a bit of a language barrier, René. When I agreed to take in as an exchange student, I figured there *would* be. It was only natural. But can you at least *try* to clean up your act? *Nettoyez-vous?* Oh, what's the use? It's only for six more months, right? Just pour that out wherever you want. I'll excavate your room when you go back to Paris.

ENDING 3

_____

_____

_____

_____

_____

_____

_____

_____

LAND OF BOILED FISH

HE. How many times do I have to *say* it? I don't *like* boiled fish! *(beat)* I *can't* eat anything else! Because – there *is* nothing else to eat! I can't go out and get a taco or Thai or curry – because we are stuck out here in the middle of Alaska with this insane *family* of yours! I'm sorry, Chaise, but you were right. They *are* insane! I didn't want to believe it, because you're so terrific and I just figured, "How bad could they *be*?" Well, they aren't just bad. They're horrible! And seeing them – and you with them...well, I hate to say it, but I think we may be incompatible. No. I'm not joking. I know we've only been married for sixteen hours, but there is a growing realization in my mind that I should have met them sooner. Who's the one without the teeth? Oh, excuse me, I'll rephrase that. "Who's the one with the really bad *fake* teeth that keep falling out?" Futon? Who would name a kid Futon? What is this furniture fetish? Is it because they don't *have* any furniture? And your father, with all those moose heads... how many moose – mooses? – *moose* – does one person need to kill? Is he going for the world's record? And that kitchen smells like a sewer! I know, I know it's the blubber, but it's awful. As soon as we landed here, I looked out at that barren tundra and I thought, "Oh, my God. I don't know anything *about* her!" Correction – I know the Florida You but I've never seen the Alaska You – the you of your past – and it's *frightening*! Why didn't you *tell* me your family was so...*primitive*? And they expect me to go to the bathroom in that – that *bucket* over there? What's wrong with a bathroom? Well, I am not going on the whale hunt, Chaise. I'm not. I'll sit here in this shack and freeze but I refuse to

go out on a canoe that your cousin Sofa made by hand
and hunt down a – a giant sea creature! I will stay here
and wait until the private plane returns on Tuesday.

ENDING 1

The way I see it is, you've got a choice to make: me
or them. I know that sounds harsh, and you're probably thinking I'm a big jerk, but I never knew anything
about this bizarre past of yours other than the hand-
ful of anecdotes you told me. As far as I'm concerned,
you're not the you I married. And I need to know right
here and now, which You *are* You?

ENDING 2

I'm not cut out for a life like this. I'm just not. I'm not
hearty and I'm not somebody who can build canoes
out of fallen trees and I'm not the kind of guy who can
eat a seal's eyeball. I know they consider it a delicacy
but I need you back in Florida with me. I will try to
endure this for a few more days...maybe I can even
stick it out for the whole week...but please, promise
me: we don't have to come up here very often. Please?
I don't think I can take it.

ENDING 3

_____
_____
_____
_____
_____
_____
_____
_____

WEDDING BELL BLUES

SHE. You're not a *husband*! A husband would care about his wife's feelings! All you care about is how much the cake cost! The cake and how many bottles of champagne were consumed and – oh, lest I forget! – making people park their own cars…in the rain…in a field foot-deep with mud…You keep tabs on everything! It was supposed to be my wedding day, Roger! My one and only, glorious wedding day and it turned out to be worse than a trip to the 99 cents store with only a quarter in my pocket. I couldn't *believe* it…you got up there and stopped the band in the middle of their last song because you didn't want them going into "overtime." Right in the middle of the father-daughter dance! I know, I know, my father's not the greatest man to ever walk the earth, but still! The father-daughter dance! And offering to "hum" the rest of the song didn't make up for it! If you haven't noticed, you're tone deaf! But that wasn't the worst of it. Because then you had the unprecedented gall to ask for a refund on the food that wasn't eaten! In case you didn't notice, they *cooked* the food, Roger! They cooked it and served it! They can't glue the beef burgundy back onto the cow or stick the peas back in the pods! *(beat)* I'm sorry daddy doesn't have any money, okay? And I'm sorry that we had to pay for our own wedding, all right? I'm sorry! But is this what the rest of my life is going to be? You, counting every nickel we spend? If so, then let me out now. Before it's too late. I could still escape! I could leap out of this car while it's still moving and you could continue on to our honeymoon all by yourself! That way, you'll win! You can stay in cheapest room at the Mountain View Inn and have only an appetizer for dinner and recoup some of the cost of this wedding!

ENDING 1

You...*what*? You...you upgraded to the Presidential Suite? Oh, Roger...I don't know what to say. Here I've been berating you for the last five minutes and...I don't know what to say! Can we get champagne, too? *(delighted:)* Oh, Roger! You do love me! *(sighs)* This is the best wedding day ever!

ENDING 2

Well, I'm sorry, but that's how I feel! You didn't *used* to act this way. Back when we were dating. Maybe you covered it up, I don't know. But after watching you today...*I'm* the one who wants a refund. I'm serious. If you keep acting this cheap all the time, we may not make it to our first anniversary! So start spending, buster. If you know what's good for our marriage!

ENDING 3

_____
_____
_____
_____
_____
_____
_____
_____

TETHERED

HE. I have driven across six states, hitchhiked through another two, walked fifty miles and practically crawled up that driveway only to find out that I never existed. I thought I had a past back there. I thought I had roots…but come to find out, I'm not really tethered to anyplace – geographically or emotionally. All these years, I thought of my mom and dad as…well, mom and dad. But to walk in that door and be told right to my face – by the woman I thought was my sister no less – that I am *not* part of their family…it makes your head spin. *(beat)* I told you how I found out, didn't I? That they died. In a newspaper. Somebody called me and asked, "Have you seen the obituaries?" I should've known when my name wasn't included in the list of surviving family members. I figured that was just good ol' big sister Carol, controlling everything like she always did…I just…I never dreamed I was adopted. I always felt like such a part of that family. My pictures were in the photo albums, along with everybody else's. I went on all the family vacations with the other kids. Why does it make me any less of a McKenzie just because I came from an orphanage? And to think that Carol would have me surgically removed from everything – including the will – just because I wasn't one of the "birth siblings"…well, I guess that was the bitterest pill to swallow. I always just took it for granted that we'd remain a family…that we'd look after each other, deep into our old age…but now I realize, I'm on my own. Part of me wants to go out and find out who my real parents are .. and the rest of me thinks it's a waste of time. I need to find my own place in the world now, LuAnn. Who I am. Where I belong.

ENDING 1

I think that we could help anchor each other. I mean, you lost your parents, too, so...I'm asking...will you come with me? You're not tied to this place any more than I am. Maybe we could find ourselves together. Hit the road, find a new town, get jobs and figure out who we are. I could do this on my own...but I'm much better with you at my side. What do you say, LuAnn? Are you ready for a journey?

ENDING 2

So I'm leaving. I know you've stuck by me through all this and I shouldn't be walking away...but I have to leave in order to find out who I really am. If we're meant to be together, then I'll be back. But I can't promise you anything until I know for sure who I am and what I want out of life.

ENDING 3

_____
_____
_____
_____
_____
_____
_____
_____

THE ME OF YESTERYEAR

SHE. I know that's not what you wanted to hear. It's just...I had hoped that you would practice some kind of restraint, Angie. That you'd be a bit more cautious, think things through...I thought you were smarter than me. But I guess we're more alike than I realized. *(beat)* I lost my virginity in a salvage yard. On the rusted-out hood of a 1974 Dodge Dart. I had rust stains on my rear for two weeks afterwards. His name was "Tube." Well, that was his nickname. I can't even remember his real name now, he was fat and sweaty and smelled like onions. Now, whenever I see a Dodge Dart...or the color rust for that matter...or chop an onion...I want to cry. Sometimes I do cry. But not from chopping an onion. I cry for that girl who was so – so *desperate* to be a woman, who was so anxious to grow up. I cry because, if I could, I would go back in time and tell her, "There's no rush! Enjoy being a kid while you can – it goes by so fast." But I can't do that. I can't go back in time. I can't talk to the me of yesteryear and I can't change my past. All I can do is try to be an example for you, Angie. And I hope I can help you change your future. No, no – I didn't talk to your mother. Please! You know me better than that. I've always been straight with you. I've always told you the truth about life, about me – about everything. So, please – if you don't listen to anybody else around you – listen to your Aunt Deb. I've been where you are right now. I can see where you're going. And I beg you, just stop and think. There's no way I can go back and change my choices...but I can at least try to help *you* make better ones.

ENDING 1

I've tried to be a good aunt. I – no, Angie, listen – I
– all right. Then *don't* listen to me. I'm only trying to
help. If I could send you back in time and stand you
beside the me of way back then, you two would be oh,
so much alike. It took me awhile to learn from my mis-
takes. I had hoped that I could help you avoid them
altogether, but I can't live your life for you. Do what
you have to, Angie. But promise me one thing: you'll
think about what I've said.

ENDING 2

I know your friends are pressuring you... I'm sure
this guy is pressuring you, too. And I'll bet the urge to
please all of 'em is overwhelming. But, Angie, the only
person you *really* have to please...is yourself. You're
not going to be harmed in any way, shape or form if
you decide to wait...but there are all kinds of harms –
physical, emotional – whatever – that can come from
rushing into this. Trust me. I know from experience.
So what'll it be, Angie? Am I getting through at all?

ENDING 3

_____
_____
_____
_____
_____
_____
_____
_____

BAD PERSON

HE. I wish I could cry. Like you. You're like a regular dripping faucet. All the time. Something happens… something good, something bad, whatever – and you just turn on like a spigot. Ten times a day, you burst out in tears. It can be something as saccharine as a Hallmark commercial…or as significant as a third world famine on the evening news. I've never seen anything like it. But me? I dunno what it is with me. No matter what happens…nothing seems to trigger any tears. My dog gets hit by a car…no tears. I get fired…no tears. One time I even tried rubbing onions into my eyes – how sick is *that*? – but that didn't work either. So tell me…how do you do it? I mean, if I were like you…then people might actually think I had emotions. Right now, everybody just assumes I'm "cold," "closed off," "out of touch," whatever. *(beat)* No, no, I'm *not* making fun of you! That's not it at all! I'm completely serious about this. You're just more "connected" than me. It's a fact. Connected with yourself… with others…you're in tune with the feelings of everybody around you. But me…I slam doors in people's faces, say rude things to them, make them feel awful – without even meaning to. It's just how I am. I'm a bad person, Cindy. I'm callous, uncaring and rotten! See that cat over there? I think of things, like, if I kicked it, you'd break out in sobs – gut-wrenching sobs. Or if I came home lying and said I'd won the lottery, you'd dissolve into sympathetic tears of joy. Either way, the tears flow. It's frustrating and it's amazing and it's… really kind of awe-inspiring.

ENDING 1

So here's my idea: I want you to be my trainer. I want you to train me to have emotions – or at least to show them. You can do whatever you want to me – whatever it takes...but I want to be a person who feels emotions rather than one who shuns them. Do you think you could help me out? *(beat)* Oh, now, don't cry. Cindy! I know you're moved, but this is really nothing to cry about! Cindy? Cindy! Oh, here we go again ...

ENDING 2

I guess you're just wired differently than me. And as a result, everybody thinks of you as kind...compassionate...caring. They just think I'm a callous jerk. So what's your secret? It's important to me to be thought of as having at least one or two emotions. So maybe you could share a secret or two? A trick? Or just be totally honest with me, once and for all: am I a bad person?

ENDING 3

_____

_____

_____

_____

_____

_____

_____

_____

CAUGHT IN A LIE

SHE. Call it what you want – but I call it a lie! *(beat)* No, I'm not exaggerating! I'm not! You told me – you said – you'd be gone. To work. Now I find out you don't even have a *job*? What else have you lied to me about? No. No. Now, stop it. I'm not! I'm *not* trying to make this about *me*. This is about *you*. I come home – will you quit getting hysterical? – I come back to my home and there you are, sitting there in that ridiculous bathrobe watching Dr. Phil or whatever it is! Is that what you've been doing all these months? Sitting around watching daytime TV and lying to me about how "great" things were at the office? Suggesting you had a promotion in the works? Oh, that is so offensive! No! That's not the point! I'm not *talking* about me! I'm not talking about the fact that I brought a man home. What this is about, is the fact that you lied! That you are clearly here when you weren't *supposed* to be here! This always happens! Always! You continually try to turn it around and make it about me, don't you? All your lies about how everybody liked you at work – it was all a load of crap, wasn't it? No, now stop trying to change the topic. You keep trying to make this about the fact that I brought Elliot home. This is not about me cheating on you, this is about you lying to me! Honestly! You are so selfish sometimes!

ENDING 1

What? You're what? *Leaving* me? How can you leave me? You're wearing a bathrobe, Duane! Calm down! Why are you so upset anyway? The way you're acting, you'd think I was the one who had lied to you or something. I – *(Pause, then she realizes she's been caught having an affair.)* Oh. You mean...Elliot. Oh, well, he's just...*Elliot*! He...I...well, I can explain. Really. Duane? Duane! Where are you going?!

ENDING 2

Okay. Okay, fine, then! *Don't* take responsibility for your actions. That's always the way with you, isn't it? You just keep talking and talking and talking about something or other that has nothing whatsoever to do with what's really going on! I swear, Duane. Sometimes I wonder why I ever trusted you in the first place!

ENDING 3

_____
_____
_____
_____
_____
_____
_____
_____

HIDDEN MOTIVE

HE. What? You woke me up to ask me *what?* What am I *thinking?* I'll tell you what I'm thinking – I'm thinking, "Why the hell did you wake me *up?!*" *That's* what I'm thinking! I – *(sighs:)* Good grief, Nanette. Now I'll *never* get back to sleep. You know what a light sleeper I am — how long it takes me to get back to… *(an idea dawns:)* Wait a minute. Wait just one minute! You did this on purpose, didn't you? You wanted me to lie awake, the rest of the night, sleepless…staring at the ceiling…I know how you think. Everything is a subtle suggestion with you, isn't it? Everything! You can't just ask somebody a simple question, there's always a Hidden Motive underneath, isn't there? *(ponders:)* So, let's see…you asked what I was thinking about…so you must want to *trick* me into thinking…of something .… I don't know what…let's see…what could it be…? Your birthday's coming up? No, that was last month. A dinner date? No, we just had one of those. What could it be? What purpose could you have for waking me up like this, knowing how damaging it would be to me, my mental state and my need for a good night's sleep? *(another idea:)* Or…maybe *you're* thinking about something. You've got something on *your* mind and you're asking me if I'm thinking about something to deflect the fact that you're preoccupied. Like *you're* the one, hiding something! Well? What are you hiding, Nanette?

ENDING 1

No! No! No, I'm not "accusing" you. I'm not accusing you of *anything*! I'm just asking – well, now, don't get all *sore*, Nanette! I just asked if maybe you were hiding something and...well, I'm sorry! I am! *(sighs:)* But you have to admit, it *is* suspicious. When a man's wife wakes him in the night to ask if he's thinking. It's suspicious because it sounds like *she's* the one doing all the thinking! So just tell me, Nanette. What did you mean when you asked me if I was thinking? *(pause)* About *what?* Our *anniversary?* Oh. Yes, well, ah...me, too.

ENDING 2

Oh, no. No. You're hiding *something*! Why else would you wake me up in the middle of the night, struggling to conceal some – some – *secret*! Some intimate secret that you don't want me to find out about! Were you lying awake, plotting to meet another man? What, then? What? *(pause)* Our *anniversary?* *(gulp)* Of course I remember. I...I...guess I was thinking about that, too.

ENDING 3

_____
_____
_____
_____
_____
_____
_____
_____

PROS AND CONS

SHE. My father always used to say, "When in doubt, make up a pro and con list." He always did it. He made one up for everything. He even made one up on the day he died. Pro: the pain will stop...I'll get to see Martha...I won't have to go to work anymore...no more bills to pay." Then the other column: "Con: I'll be leaving Jenny all alone." *(beat)* Well, obviously, the pro's won. He let go and died just ten minutes after making up that list. *(pause)* He was quite a guy. He pretty much ingrained that whole "pro and con" thing in me, so I seem to find myself making up my own lists now. I still remember vividly the one I made up when I met you. Pros: he's a great guy...he's a great guy...he's a really great guy. Cons: well...none. So now I find myself making up yet another pro and con list. *(holds out a piece of paper)* The pros are...being with you...a new job for you...the chance to see the world...did I mention being with you? Well, the "con" side makes it a bit more complicated...being away from my girls... leaving Boston...saying good-bye to all my friends...my job...giving up that great, great apartment that took seven years to find...there's more, but those are the "highlights." *(beat)* I thought it would all be so black and white, y'know, that would all be so *clear.* The cons win, right? But it's not that simple. Then it hit me ...

ENDING 1

You outweigh anything on a list. You are the most important thing that's ever happened to me and if a pro and con list says you're not important, well then to hell with logical reasoning. My heart feels like I'm meant to be with you, and for the first time in my life, I'm going to follow my heart and not some stupid list. Don't look so serious! I'm *happy*! And *this*...is a moment to celebrate!

ENDING 2

My life really is here. But you have to find yours. Maybe it will turn out to be back here, with me, I certainly don't know and who could say? One day, maybe you'll be back. And if your path leads you back here to me of its own accord...well, then maybe we were meant to be. But for now, I have to go with the tried and true method. The pro's and con's say it all. And I have to listen to them. I'm sorry, Dean. But that's just how I seem to work...and that's where I stand.

ENDING 3

_____
_____
_____
_____
_____
_____
_____
_____

THE CAVE-IN

HE. I used to be a ventriloquist. I got expelled from the Canadian Association of Ventriloquist Entertainers – CAVE, as we call it – for moving my lips. I was doing a birthday party in Ottawa when all of a sudden…I don't know exactly what happened…but my dummy Murray was making a joke – and all of a sudden, everybody was staring at me strangely. Even the kids. I'd always heard about that look from those guys in the CAVE retirement home but I'd never actually seen it before. The first rule of CAVE is, don't CAVE in – meaning, don't shatter the illusion that the dummy is the one doing the talking. Pretty obvious, huh? You learn that on Day One, when they make you watch all these horrific old videos of ventriloquists with their lips moving. *(shudders at the memory)* Anyway, the kids started hurling things at me…slices of birthday cake…presents…a piñata…I fled from the party as fast as I could. It was only after I'd driven nine miles that I realized, I'd left Murray behind. All of a sudden, I'd violated the two cardinal rules: don't CAVE in and don't leave your dummy behind. I went back, but I was too late. I hid in the bushes and watched in horror as those cute little kids tore Murray limb-from-limb… *(fights back tears:)* … then they took his disembodied trunk…stuffed it with hard candies…and made him the piñata! *(cries)* Oh, don't. Don't, Susan. Don't ask me to go out there and do it again. I know it was a huge part of my past, but I just can't!

ENDING 1

What? Of *course* I love you! This is not about *you*! It's about my failure to – what? Oh, please don't blackmail me like this. I mean, I'd do anything for you, but… don't ask me to do this one thing. I know. I know you're testing me. You're trying to see if I'm the man you want to spend the rest of your life with. But I beg you, test me in any way you see fit – but not this! *Anything* but ventroliquism!

ENDING 2

I can't. I'd rather hide in the shadows than shrivel in the spotlight. I know you must look at me and think that's pitiful. That I'm not the person I used to be. But we all adapt, don't we? Adapt to changing circumstances, changing situations, changing times. I've adapted, that's all. Adapted to a new world in which ventriloquism plays no part anymore.

ENDING 3

_____
_____
_____
_____
_____
_____
_____
_____

STATUS SYMBOLS

SHE. When did you become such an elitist snob? No, I'm serious! You ought to hear yourself talk. It's endless! All you've done for the past ten or fifteen minutes is rant about how much things cost! It's *so* self-serving! You used to care about other things and other people, but now...all you ever talk about is how much you have in the stock market or what your suit cost or how many maids you have. And don't even get me started about that ridiculous car of yours! Who in their right mind needs a $250,000 car?! *(beat)* No, they're not "status symbols," Stuart. They're mirrors of your vanity. The only thing they symbolize is how full of yourself you've become. What happened to the humble older brother I knew back in Beaverton? You used to hitch rides around town. Or walk. I'll bet you wouldn't be caught *dead* walking anyplace these days. The other day, Fran said you actually started the car, opened the garage and drove one house down to ask your next door neighbor for a drill. And that was only because your $2,000 Swiss one wasn't working! What happened, Stuart? We were both raised in the same house, with the same parents and yet you've turned out to be...well, a rich, snobby jerk! You look down on everybody who doesn't earn six figures, and – what?

ENDING 1

I'm not ranting! I'm *not*! Believe it or not, I'm actually about to make a *point* here. Which is...and this is hard to say...but I don't want Bradley coming over here anymore. He's only ten years old, but I can already see a difference in him. Whenever he comes back from your house, he's not the same kid. He acts spoiled, sullen... mean. He thinks you're the coolest uncle, but it's not worth it if he gets corrupted in the process. I'm sorry, Stuart. But I have to draw the line. I'm the Mama Bear. And I have to guard what's mine.

ENDING 2

Well, I'm sorry if you think of me as one of the "poor people"...but I consider myself to be much wealthier than you are. When it comes to having a sense of what's important in life, and what matters most, I am infinitely richer than you will ever be! I have a family that I put above everything else in the world – above any price – can you say the same?

ENDING 3

_____
_____
_____
_____
_____
_____
_____
_____

TIRADE

HE. Aaaghhhh! If you don't stop jabbering, I don't know *what* I'll do! I might just put my head through the wall or fling myself out the window! It's like this squeaking wheel, this unending stream of, "blah, blah, blah, did you hear what happened to blah, blah, blah, and then what happened was, blah, blah blah ..." and on and on and on! Don't you *ever* stop talking? No! No, that's not true. You talk in your sleep, too! *(pause)* There! For *one moment*! You stopped! *(sighs:)* Sheer *ecstasy*! I tell you, Diane. I don't know if I can take it much longer – this endless stream of banality that flows out of your mouth like sewage down a drain. I have to confess, I've actually fantasized about finding some unethical eye, ear, nose and throat specialist and sneaking him in here in the dead of night and having him snip your vocal chords! Not that I would actually go through with it, but I sure do think about it! Why? Because I can't hear myself think because of your continuous outpour of babble! Stream of consciousness is all well and good, Diane, but trust me – nobody – *nobody* needs to narrate every moment of their life! Nobody needs to voice their inner thoughts like you do! They're thoughts that may be completely compelling to you, but they're painful for everybody else – which, most of the time, is me!

ENDING 1

I don't know what the solution is. Ernie suggested that I try wearing ear plugs, and – *(beat)* What? Well, of course I talked it over with Ernie, he's my brother, for cryin' out loud! He thought maybe ear plugs would help. I said, sure, at night, but what about during the day? And then he said maybe I could have my ear drums punctured and we could both learn sign language…which wouldn't be the worst thing in the world but I really got frightened when I imagined you babbling with your hands! So what do we do here, Diane? I really need your help on this one. How can I make you stop talking?!

ENDING 2

I'm sorry it's come to this, Diane… I know we've had this conversation time and again…but until you can find some way to stop talking 24 hours a day, you're gonna have to get used to the feeling of duct tape on your mouth. I'm sorry, but it's the only way to solve this sticky situation. Now close your mouth and get ready… because here it comes. And I bought "extra-sticky," too!

ENDING 3

_____

_____

_____

_____

_____

_____

_____

_____

DECLARATION OF WAR

SHE. Don't give me that look. There! "That" look! All I asked was – no, no! What I asked was, "Could you please pick up those filthy, disgusting underpants?" *You're* the one who flew into a rage, not me! I have left them sitting there – on the coffee table, mind you – for two weeks now! I've tip-toed past them…I've held my nose as I've passed…and I've been watching…waiting…wondering how long it would be before you noticed them. And you haven't! If I hadn't pointed them out just now, I guess you would've assumed that they were part of the décor, huh? Right. Like, I'm re-doing the entire house in "Poop Streak Moderne." It's not like I'm asking you to do any more than you already do. I've accepted the fact that you're not going to clean up the house on the weekends. You work hard, Stan, I realize that. So I do it all. Everything that has to be done in this big, huge house. But last time I checked, this was a marriage, not a "who works the hardest" contest! We're a partnership. And partners help each other. Look, I know in every relationship there are battles. And there are hills that you decide you'll die on. Well, this is my hill. Underwear hill is the hill I will definitely die on. So I'm asking…nicely…again…could you *please* pick up your dirty underwear? *(pause)*

ENDING 1

No? All right, then. Fine. You may think you've won the battle, but I swear you will lose the war. That's right. You just started yourself a war, mister! Wait 'til I pull out the heavy artillery. You think *you* can be dirty and disgusting? You just wait! When your office is filled to overflowing with feminine hygiene products, you'll be begging to surrender! And I don't take prisoners!

ENDING 2

See? That wasn't so bad, was it? Now...no! Don't put them on the television! Good grief, Stan! The whole point was to move them out of the room! To the laundry bin – or the trash can – not to another clean surface! Honestly! How in the world am I ever going to teach you *not* to live in your own filth? I don't want this to escalate into an all-out war between us...do *you?*

ENDING 3

_____

_____

_____

_____

_____

_____

_____

_____

BIG DAN

HE. When I realized how much trouble I'd gotten myself into, my first idea was to kill myself. No, seriously. I wondered, what's the best way to do myself in? I thought, well, I could hang myself. I could throw a rope up over a good strong tree limb and – *(indicates hanging himself:)* – that'd be it. But the more I thought of it, the whole idea of rope burn really put me off. So then I thought about drinking some kind of poison…but the whole notion of swallowing a toxic chemical made me sick to my stomach. Then, when I was out in the woods with Chester, I saw that chainsaw that Emmett Stubbs left behind. I said to myself, "Now, there's an idea." I could start it up, fall on it, and cut my head off. But if I missed – if I didn't fall exactly on my neck – who knows what would happen. I might wind up slicing off an arm or something. And who knows whether a chain saw can even cut through bone? Besides, it was gas-powered and there was no gas left it in. So, after stewing and fretting and pondering this dilemma all weekend, I decided I would come see you. Big Dan. You and I have never seen eye-to-eye and I figured, well, if I just climb that mountain and bang on Dan's door and wake him up and start cussing at him…at *you*, I mean…why, you'd haul off and kill me, or throw me over the cliff, and I wouldn't *have* to kill myself! So…just now, I've called you all the names I can think of and you're not even makin' a move at me. So what do I need to do to get you riled up?

ENDING 1

Now, Dan...Dan! Don't go gettin' all pacifist on me now! I need you to haul off and *kill* me! Tear me limb from limb. Hurl me into the abyss! I'll do whatever you need – insult you, offend you or haul off and hit you... though you're so much bigger'n me, you probably won't even feel it. What do you say? Can't you lend a few lousy minutes to kill a guy like me?

ENDING 2

Whoa! Easy, big boy! I don't want you to simply maul me. I want you to make sure I'm dead. I couldn't stand waking up in some hospital to realize I'd only been maimed...this is an all-or-nothing proposition here. So, what do you say? Are you up to the task, big fella? There's an extra fifty in it for you if you make it quick and painless.

ENDING 3

_____

_____

_____

_____

_____

_____

_____

_____

COLD HANDS, WARM HEART

SHE. How could you "forget" to mention something like that? Honestly, Mort! How many times have I asked you, "What do you do for a living?" And now that I think back on it, you always managed to change the subject! No, you did! You did! Oh, what I fool I was! I see that now! I went and fell for you and now I find out – what? Yes, I fell for you, isn't it painfully obvious? Now everything is spoiled! Ruined! Tainted! It is! Because every time you touch me with those cold, cold hands, I'll wonder…whose *body* were they on today? *(reacts angrily)* No, that's not "stupid." You're a mortician, Mort! You handle dead people all day long. Make them up. Pose them. How am I supposed to feel when the hands that sculpted their final resting poses reach out for *me*? *(shivers)* Ugh, I get goose bumps all over my body just imagining it! Don't say it. Because. I know what you're going to say. "Cold hands, warm heart." And I *know* you have a warm heart, Mort. Really, I do, I know that. You have the warmest heart of probably anybody I know. But I don't know if I can get past the cold hands thing! And no. Gloves won't help. I don't want you to be wearing gloves when you embrace me! Especially not plastic ones!

ENDING 1

If you love me…really, really love me…then maybe it's time to start thinking about a new line of work. I know it's a lot to ask, but, hey – wouldn't you find it more interesting to work with *living* people all day long? Or maybe you like the fact that they don't talk back to you…at any rate, I hope you'll at least think about it. Because I don't believe I can take your "cold hands" that much longer.

ENDING 2

Mort, I can't believe I'm going to say this, because you're such a really swell guy in so many, many ways… but I think I have to let you go. I know, I know, it's crazy, but I don't want it to suddenly be twenty years later and I've never let you touch me and we're old and miserable and hating each other. Really. If you step back and look at it from my point of view…breaking up might be the most reasonable thing we can do. And I'm nothing if not reasonable…right?

ENDING 3

_____
_____
_____
_____
_____
_____
_____
_____

BOLD STEP TODAY

HE. *(nursing his nose:)* Is it broken? I think it may be broken. He really hauled off and wailed on me, didn't he? *(strikes a pose)* So, how do I look? Like Jake LaMotta? You know, the guy in *Raging Bull*? He had a broken nose, didn't he? *(feels his nose, cautiously.)* It's not crooked, is it? I don't think it's crooked. Anyway, I'd say I came out of this thing pretty well, all things considered. Wouldn't you? I mean, I had no idea if Vern was gonna be violent or dangerous and yet I walked right up to him and said, "Your wife is in love with me." That should score some points with you, Beaula. That should show you that I mean business. I've been trying to find a way to prove to you that I love you, and walking up to your ex-husband – whom you admit yourself to be the most jealous and possessive man alive – and telling him that I love you…well, that's an act of courage, wouldn't you say? You've been waiting for me to show you an act of courage. That's what I did today. *(sniffs and snorts a few times)* I can't breathe out of it quite right…maybe it's just swollen. Does it look swollen? Or does it look broken? No matter. I told a bold step today, Beaula, and – what? No! I'm not making this about "me." It's all about you! My love for you. So I guess it's about both me and you, but still. I can't believe you would say that. What do you think I am, some kind of *egomaniac*? For the last time – this isn't about me! It's about you. Well, you and me. Or, rather, me and you and how crazy I am about you!

ENDING 1

What? No! *(then, realizes:)* Well...maybe you're right. Maybe I *have* made this about me! Wow. I never realized before...but...I'm a pretty amazing guy! To think that I would be the kind of fella to walk up to Vern and confront him like that – I'm brave! I never thought of myself as brave before, but I guess I am! *(beat)* For the last time – *no*! I am not making this about "me!" This is – and always *has* been – all about you!

ENDING 2

Beaula! I just walked up to your ex-husband and insulted him! I did it for you! How dare you throw that back in my face and tell me I don't care about you! Or whatever you were saying. If I didn't care about you, why would I risk getting my face pounded in? I swear – and I mean this, now – I would get my face pounded in each and every day if it meant I could spend the rest of my life with you. *(beat)* But for now...could you please get me some ice? My nose is starting to throb.

ENDING 3

_____

_____

_____

_____

_____

_____

_____

_____

LIFE AND DEATH

SHE. That is *not* what I said! I said – no, what I *said* was, and I quote: "Look over there. I used to date that guy. He was such a jerk." I didn't say "Hey, kill that guy, would you?" Somehow – on your own – in that agitated brain of yours – you took my comment, "He was such a jerk," and translated it into, "Hey, kill that guy, would you?" What? Well, it's too late now! He's dead! No, I am not wishing I was still with him! Ugh! You are so thick sometimes! And this is not about the fact that we saw him mugging some old lady. Okay, he's a mugger. He's a scumbag. He's a bad guy. I get it. The truth of the matter is, I'm in genuine shock that (a) somebody I know is dead and (b) somebody *else* I know – namely you – killed him with your bare hands! *(sighs)* Y'know…I honestly thought I could deal with this whole thing about your work. You told me, on our first date, you said it. "I'm a trained assassin." And I stupidly thought, "That can't be much different from any other nine to five job." Boy, was I wrong! I thought I could live with the immorality of it all…but I can't. I know, I know, you think it's "moral" if you're doing it for a government power, but that – just now – was *not* for a government power! That was a guy named Rick whom you beat to death with a garbage can lid! Where would you even learn to *use* a garbage can lid as a weapon?! What, like, spy school? Oh, excuse me. High school. Whatever. The point is, now what am I supposed to do? I could almost deal with this job of yours when it was just a concept, but now that I've seen you "at work," so to speak…it's *real*! It's visceral! And it's totally freaking me out!

ENDING 1

I mean, if we go through with this – if I say "I do" tomorrow – then how do I know you won't kill your best man? Or my maid of honor? When does the killing stop?! *(calms herself)* I'm sorry...I guess I got carried away. It's just...I don't want to end up on your "hit list," all right? So if I ever do anything to upset you, or offend you, or make you angry...tell me right away. When I say, "'Til death do us part," I want to really mean by natural causes!

ENDING 2

What? What do you mean, I'm the only one? I'm the only person you ever let witness a murder? Oh, well, gee – thanks! I don't know what to say. "I'm honored" just doesn't seem to cut it. The weird thing is...you're such a great guy in most respects...why do you have to be a trained killer as well? Why couldn't you have been a shop owner or a mechanic? I know, I know. Then you wouldn't be "you." I just don't know what to do...and running into Rick sure didn't help!

ENDING 3

_____
_____
_____
_____
_____
_____
_____
_____

FRIENDLY FIRE

HE. Can it, soldier! That's not a suggestion, it's an *order*! Enough of this crap, now snap out of it! *(beat; then softening a bit:)* Look...it *happens*, all right? You've got to – listen to me! – you've got to let it go! I just said – these things happen! They happen to you and to me and everybody else! Did you ever wonder why I limp? It's because I've got this tiny little fragment of shrapnel embedded in my knee that no surgeon has ever been able to remove! There's not a day on earth that I don't feel the pain – and it was all because of a guy in my unit. He freaked out and fired into a metal staircase — the thing shattered...and down I went. Ironic that they call it "friendly fire." There's nothing friendly about it. But do I carry a grudge? No. I let it go a long time ago and moved on. Because in the midst of a firefight – listen to me – in the midst of a firefight, when all the shit's going down – and I don't care who tells you they know what's what and who's who, no matter how experienced they are. It's total chaos. When the bullets start raining down on you and you're diving for cover and you're trying to save your life and the lives of your friends...it isn't always cut and dried. People react, soldiers react and sometimes they react too quickly or not quickly enough...whatever. The point is, it happens. It's one of the side effects of this whole messy business we call war. We can get you counseling, if you want it. We can ship you home on leave, if you want. But nobody can take away the sense of self-blame. Only you and you alone can do that.

ENDING 1

You're the best sharpshooter I've got in this unit, and I'd like nothing better than to take you with me when we go into that village tomorrow. I know what you're going through – believe me, I've been there. You wounded a guy. One of ours. It was an accident. I understand. Now, if you can find a way to put that aside and come with us...we've got a battle to fight. And if you can't...then it's time for you to ship out. So... what's it gonna be, soldier? Think before you answer – because I won't ask twice.

ENDING 2

I won't pretend that it's easy. I've seen firsthand what it can do to you. *(beat)* We were on a routine patrol... ambushed... Charlie Wyatt's firearm discharged and killed his friend Ned Curtis from Pittsburgh. His C.O. forgave him. But he couldn't forgive himself. That's when he started drinking. And he never stopped... until he woke up dead one morning. So you see? You gotta let it go before it takes control of you once and for all.

ENDING 3

_____
_____
_____
_____
_____
_____
_____
_____

EXPECTATIONS

SHE. I think everybody around me would be a whole lot happier if they just lowered their expectations a little. I mean, I just seem to disappoint *everybody* sooner or later, so maybe if they didn't expect so much out of me, everything would turn out fine! Don't you think? I sure do. *(beat)* Like Aunt Irmagard. She kept going on and on about how much she wanted a Lemon Ice Box Pie. So I finally made her one. Trouble is, it turned out something awful. The meringue looked like piled up pigeon poop and the pie itself tasted like a wad of chewed-up lemons wrapped in crackers. I tried like crazy; I just don't know how to make exotic desserts like that. Or when Old Man Odom asked if I could house-sit for him. Only thing was, he had nine cats. And by the time he got back, only two were still alive! If he had only said, "I don't expect 'em all to survive in my absence" or something – well then he wouldn't have been so disappointed in me. Point is, everybody's disappointed in me, some way or another. Momma just clucks her tongue, turns away and gazes out the window whenever I walk through the room. And Daddy...well, he's stopped even returning my phone calls. I think he's afraid I'm a jinx and something bad'll happen to him if he hears my voice. *(beat)* So the way I see it, I got two choices: one, get everybody else to lower their expectations. That way, they won't be all upset when I goof things up. Or two, go see the Voodoo Woman out on Wompat Road and get her to find out if there's a curse on me. Maybe there is, and maybe there's some way she can lift it.

ENDING 1

They say she helped old Archibald Harvey get his hearing back after that shotgun went off next to his ear... and that she gave Loretta Jugg a love potion that made Mr. Colon Graham propose marriage to her on first sight! Now, I know our family tends to look down on Voodoo Magic...but I don't see any other way out. I got to go talk to the Voodoo Woman...or all those around me are positively doomed!

ENDING 2

Why am I telling you all this? Because...I'm crazy about you, Billy! I really and truly am. I'm just afraid if I say "yes," and we get married, I'll only disappoint you in the end. So either I should say "no" and disappoint you...or you should totally lower your expectations of me as a wife. Because I don't want to disappoint you. You matter way, way too much to me.

ENDING 3

_____
_____
_____
_____
_____
_____
_____
_____

LITERARY CARNIVORE

HE. Ugh! I wish Squirt would leave me alone. Who? Oh, Squirt. That's his name. Well, what we *call* him, anyway. I've given nicknames to just about everybody on the sixteenth floor. I call him "Squirt" because we caught him hunkered down in the handicapped stall of the men's room with horrendous diarrhea one day…then there's Bowser, the jowly fellow at the end of the hall – we saw him practically French-kissing his dog one afternoon…and of course let's not forget Flea Boy, that scrawny little guy with glasses who sits near the window, who looks like he's always picking fleas off of himself…and so forth and so on. You get the idea. I guess you might say I'm the resident expert at handing out monikers. Nicknames. Funny slogans. Whenever a new person starts working here, the guys start to scrutinize them for weird traits and then they come to me to ask me to generate a nickname. It's a special skill of mine. *(pause)* What do you mean? *(laughs)* No! That's absurd. Of course, I don't have a nickname. Because. *I'm* the one who makes up all the nicknames, why would I have one if… *(pause)* What do you mean? They have a nickname for *me?* The…wait a minute, the people on this floor…my friends…they've cooked up a nickname for me? Well, what is it? *(a long, incredulous pause)* "Viper"? Well, that's ridiculous! That doesn't even make any sense! Why, a viper is something that attacks its prey, and…oh, my. *(disillusioned:)* Is that how they see me? As some kind of, of literary carnivore who attacks the weaker-minded?

ENDING 1

Good Lord, I never thought of these people as my "prey." And yet... *(pause)* They're right. I *do* attack them. All of them. Nobody's sacred. Even my boss, he... *(suddenly paranoid:)* He doesn't know we call him "Poop Breath," does he? Good. Good. Then there's still time to turn the tide. I've got to start coming up with nicer nicknames, Nora. Because sooner or later, the prey rebels!

ENDING 2

Well, it serves them right! All of them! Why was I put on earth if not to zero-in on the truth and point it out for everybody to see? It's not like I'm *lying*. I'm only showing them their foibles. Blemishes. Foul characteristics. It's only to be expected that they'd lash back at me in some pathetic, juvenile way. But they'll see...I'm the master moniker maker...and I always win!

ENDING 3

_____

_____

_____

_____

_____

_____

_____

_____

ACT OF LOVE

SHE. I don't know what to say, Reverend. I don't know what to say at all. Look, I realize you're mad, but I was only borrowing your office. I just needed a quiet place to take my boyfriend for a few minutes where we could – what? Inappropriate? Well, where are we supposed to go? To *my* house? My dad would skin Eric alive and hang him on the clothesline if he found us together. My dad hates Eric! So, you see, we had to find a quiet place where we could be alone…and, well…your office is always as quiet as a tomb, so we figured you wouldn't mind! Why? Because! You're always preaching about love and loving one another and I said, okay, if he really believes in love, I want to show Eric that I love him, so I took him to your office and now there's this whole big drama and everybody's all upset! *(pause)* No! That's not true! I didn't volunteer to help out here just so's I could borrow your office! Gosh! How could you think *that*? I volunteered to help out here so's I could get out of my house and away from my dad every evening! Well – now you know! It wasn't out of any sense of duty or faith or whatever. I just needed a place to go. I mean, I didn't mind helping…and I was kind of hoping that maybe I was scoring some kind of, I dunno, bonus points with the big man upstairs by helping you out. I mean, after all, you are a minister and everything. But you can't preach about love all the time and talk to people about loving one another and then come down hard on somebody when you find them doing just that!

ENDING 1

(pause) Well, I'm sorry if that's how you feel. I don't see it that way at all. It's not a betrayal. In fact, I think you're over-reacting...but that's just me. No, no, I understand. You won't see me around here again. I just...I hope you'll think about this. And think about the message you're sending to everybody. Because if you preach love as a wonderful thing and then, as soon as you see it expressed, call it a bad thing...I think you're giving everyone a mighty mixed message!

ENDING 2

Look. I probably should have *told* you up front, all right? I just assumed...that you were on my side. And maybe you are, in your own way. But like it or not, Eric and I are getting married. I had actually hoped that you would be the one to marry us, Reverend. But after this...I don't know if I want that anymore.

ENDING 3

_____

_____

_____

_____

_____

_____

_____

_____

MOMENT OF IMPACT

HE. I never thought of myself as a praying man…but something like this really changes the way you see things. It makes you look beyond yourself for answers. *(beat)* Everybody always talks about "the accident." But the thing is, I barely even remember it. All I have is this fleeting image of myself driving, then this, this microsecond of looking to the left and seeing a truck – the grill of a truck – just inches away from my face…and that's it. Everything from the moment of impact on has somehow been erased. Forgotten. Buried in the back of my brain somewhere. Maybe it'll come back one day…maybe not. But it doesn't matter. The point is, it's been six months now. They said I'd only have two. They said I wouldn't be able to talk. Well… aren't words coming out of my mouth? And, to top it all off, they pretty much assured me I'd never walk again. Well, just moments ago I lurched all the way down the hall to that vending machine and bought myself a Mars bar. Now, you tell me that prayers aren't answered. *(pause)* Look…recovery is going to be a long haul. But I'm ready to fight. What I need to know is, are you going to be in my corner? I know it must've been…well…*freaky,* to see me all busted up like that. To see me as a shell of what I used to be. But I promise you, Dana, I'll be the me I was before. Better. Because not only will my body be healed, but my mind will be, too. I see a bigger picture of myself than I used to be. Before, I was just narrowly focused on *me,* what the world owed *me,* everything was all about *me.* Well, now I realize that we have something to give back to the world. I want to give back. And I hope you do, too.

ENDING 1

Up 'til now, our lives have been only focused on our own selfish self interests. I want to change all that. I need to know that you're willing to change with me. I think we can be better people...and we can make this world a better place. What do you say, Dana? Are you ready to take that journey with me?

ENDING 2

I realize that this is a different "me" from what you're used to. It may not be the "me" you want to spend the rest of your life with. We always were pretty hedonistic. But we can change all that. We can start fresh. We can – *(pause)* No. No, I understand. I didn't mean to throw you such a huge curve, Dana. You...you need to follow your own path. And I need to follow mine.

ENDING 3

_____

_____

_____

_____

_____

_____

_____

_____

DOG PERSON

SHE. Oh, no. I think it's perfectly clear. It's clear to *me*, at any rate! You're not a Dog Person at all! You *told* me you were a Dog Person when we met, but you were only lying! Oh, yes, you did! You did! That very first day, when we met in the park…I was walking Chester and I remember, I was bending over to pick up his poop and you said, "Nice dog." But you were probably just looking at my chest and didn't even notice Chester! It's all coming clear to me now! How you manipulated me…how you never wanted to come over to my place. Because that way you could avoid him! How you never wanted to join me when I was planning to walk him. *(realizes:)* You *hate* Chester, don't you? But…more than that…you hate all dogs! I see that now! You got sick the day we were supposed to go to the Dog Show. Yeah, well, you *never* get sick, Ernie! *Never*! It was just so you could avoid all the dogs! Well, at least I was honest. I told you, from day one, I'm a Dog Person! I said, very clearly, that a man could *only* be my soul mate if he was a Dog Person, too! And you said, "Hey, that's *me*! I'm definitely a Dog Person!" But now I see, you just said that to get to me! It was all lies! You telegraphed the truth to me just now when you refused to pet that cute little Terrier. All he wanted was a little attention! And you pulled your hand away like the dog had cooties or something and you glanced over at me real quick to see if I noticed. Well, I noticed, Ernie! I noticed that you are a big, fat liar!

ENDING 1

No. No, I don't believe you. You'll say anything to get me back. I don't believe for one minute… *(pause)* Really? All right, then. You want to prove your love to me? Then prove it. I challenge you to go work five eight-hour shifts at the shelter. Yes, the *animal* shelter. Handling dogs! If you can do that, well, then maybe I'll give you a second chance. Maybe. But you've got to prove that you're a Dog Person, Ernie…or you've got no chance with me!

ENDING 2

Stop talking! Stop it! Stop! Because there is nothing you can say that I want to hear anymore! Everything that comes out of your mouth is lies, so this is just a lie too. You're not going to "change." People can't just "change." They either like dogs, or they don't. And you obviously *don't*. Well, as far as I'm concerned, this relationship is over, Ernie! No, I mean it! You had your chance! And now…*you're* in the doghouse!

ENDING 3

_____
_____
_____
_____
_____
_____
_____
_____

EXPLOSIVE REVENGE

HE. Wait! Don't move. Don't even breathe. The box you're holding…yes, that one. Shh. Don't move. That box… there's a bomb inside! *(pause)* What? No, I'm not being ridiculous! Sheila, I'm being totally serious. Yes, I am. I am. "How would I know?" Believe me, I know! Because! I put it in there! *(pause)* Okay. This is a little bit awkward. But just listen to me very carefully…and nobody will get hurt. All right. Here's my explanation: I was mad. All right? Angry. Very upset with you because you set my hair on fire and flooded my apartment – let me finish! *(continues to explain:)* I tried to figure out some way to get even with you and somehow I settled on this idea. Right. A bomb. I met this guy down at the bar and he said, "I know how to build a bomb!" And I thought, "Hey, a bomb…okay." I know it wasn't the smartest decision, but that's all water under the bridge now. Then I came to find out that you weren't the one who set my hair on fire and that it was Jimmy LaRue who flooded my apartment and…well, I'm sorry, Sheila. Sorry for not trusting you. I love you and I want to spend the rest of my life with you but…well, there's the little matter of that bomb you're holding. But not to worry. I'll call the bomb maker and he'll tell us how to defuse it and then we'll go on just like before and everything will be fine, okay? *(beat)* What do you mean, "It can't?" I said I'd defuse the freakin' bomb, all right? Geez! You act like I'm being threatening or something! I'm trying to help you defuse a bomb here! I'm trying to save your life! And you treat me like I'm the enemy!

ENDING 1

This is why I jumped to conclusions, Sheila. This is why I naturally assumed that you set my hair on fire and flooded my apartment! Because! You're always treating me like I'm the enemy! I'm your boyfriend, Sheila! Somebody you should trust! So just come over here... and we'll get Marwan on the phone and everything will be fine. What?! Well, fine, then! Take your chances with the bomb squad, Sheila! From this moment on... you and I are *through*!

ENDING 2

Look. I've never been good with words...but I do want to apologize, Sheila. For being a jerk and telling you what to do and not trusting you...and, yes...having some guy I met in a bar build a bomb and send it to you. But I promise you, If we can just get that bomb defused, everything will work out fine. So...are you willing to trust me? Good. Bring it over here. And for God's sake...don't drop it!

ENDING 3

_____
_____
_____
_____
_____
_____
_____
_____

BEHIND THE WALL

SHE. I *need* this, Karen. I know that sounds ridiculous to you, but I so need this. Desperately. My life is such a wreck and...I don't even know how it got that way. Carl just started coming home from work later and later...I stopped making anything for him to eat for dinner... we both just kind of stopped talking to one another... and drifted into these...separate lives. We both live at the same address, obviously, but we have entirely opposite existences now. I don't really know how it all began – if he started avoiding me or I started trying to punish him. But I'm sure my withdrawing from him was a form of punishment. However it began, one action just sort of fueled another and each of us kept building up walls and now...here we are. I haven't even seen Carl in over a month. I don't call him or leave notes for him...I don't even know if he has the same job anymore! I do know that he pays the bills. I can go online and see that the phone, gas and electric have all been paid. I've even thought of asking him for a divorce, but conversation seems...impossible. Sometimes I step outside of myself, like a spectator, and look at what I've become and it's...it's so absurd! Maybe that's why I try to keep myself so busy. I mean, if I didn't have the country club and this, the fundraising drive...I would have nothing. I know that probably sounds pathetic to you, Karen. Your life is so, so... "together"...but these are the things I live with, day in and day out. I beg you not to take the chairmanship away from me. I know Lucille wants to do it, but as desperate as it sounds...this committee is all I've got left. If I didn't have that to fill my hours, my days...I honestly think I'd go crazy. I know we've never really been that close and we seldom see eye-to-eye, but please...I am begging you...don't take this away from me.

ENDING 1

I know you were disappointed with what we raised last year but if you give me a chance, I'll make it up to you, I swear! We'll double what we took in before! We'll... *(pause)* I see. Well. Maybe it's all for the best. Maybe it's time I looked at where I am...and how I got here. Maybe it's time I actually I spoke to my husband.

ENDING 2

Look. I hate to ask for anything. In some ways, I'd rather die than ask you for a favor, Karen. But please, just think about this...and give me one more chance. I will funnel all my frustration, all my energy, all my life, into this job. I know I can make a difference. Please, please, let me try.

ENDING 3

_____
_____
_____
_____
_____
_____
_____
_____

FUN & GAMES

HE. Being a superhero isn't **all** fun and games. People see you on the cover of *People* magazine and they think, "I could do that." But what they don't realize is, there's a huge element of risk involved. *You* try leaping from one building to another. If you don't aim just right – boom! Down you go, like a sack of nails. You think it doesn't hurt? Believe me, it hurts! *(chuckles)* I mean, it's not like I can *fly* or anything! *(reacting to a statement about his cape:)* I know, I know, people see the cape and figure I can float in mid-air or something, but it's not as simple as that. *(shrugs)* Strength. I do have strength. Lots of it. Oh, and I can melt things by staring at them, I tend to forget about that. But ya have to focus like crazy, and you have to stare for a long period of time to actually melt real metal. Things don't just melt right away! I remember, that one bad guy...what was his name? Oh, the Meddler! He had locked those people in a bank safe and I had to melt the lock to get 'em out...and I *did* it...but it took, like, five minutes to burn through the steel. Oy, what a headache I had *that* night! But the hardest thing of all, I think, is interpreting my mission statement. All I know is that I'm here "to help mankind." *(shrugs)* Help them...help them *what?* See what I mean? It's too vague! Talk about generalizations! I spend most of my time wrestling with that statement. The only legacy my dad left me. I wish he'd given me a spaceship or heat ray lessons but no... he gives me that one-liner, and now I have to spend the rest of my life, trying to live up to it! *(sighs)* I know I should be grateful. I mean, there are plenty of guys who'd kill to have bullets bounce off of 'em.

ENDING 1

It's just...I'm gonna age about half as fast as you do, Zelda. When you're eighty, I'll be forty-five. When you're a hundred, I'll be fifty-one. See the problem? I'm head over heels for you...but even though we're the same age now, I'm afraid I'm gonna turn out to be too young for you down the line. And I want you to know that you are the most beautiful woman I've ever met...but if I stare at you too much...I might... you know...*melt* you. And I'd hate to do that. Because you are very, very special to me.

ENDING 2

It's just...some days, I wish I could trade jobs with a guy who flips burgers or some poor schmuck who sweeps the street. What do they have to worry about? Getting their job done and punching out after eight hours. Me? I'm a 24-hour-a-day kind of guy. Which is okay, since I only need one hour of sleep...but you get the point, right? *(which is:)* Basically, I'm a regular Joe in a Super Hero body.

ENDING 3

_____
_____
_____
_____
_____
_____
_____
_____

FEELING BATTY

SHE. I've never told anybody this before…but I'm a vampire. *(pause)* You're not supposed to *laugh*! It's true! All right, go on and laugh. But if we don't break up in the next three weeks for some other reason, and we're still together at the end of the month, when the moon is full again…you'll see. No, now, that's a myth. People don't turn into werewolves during a full moon, people turn into vampires during a full moon. Well, you'll see. You think you know everything, but you don't. When you get right down to it, Richard, that may be the biggest problem you and I have – not that I'm a vampire – well, I guess "vampiress" is the proper term – the fact that you always think you're right. There's never any room for *me* to be right, you don't make an allowance for it. It's true! Like the other day, when I told you you'd set your hair on fire if you tried to light the gas grill with a paper match. I told you, I said, you need one of those really long matches, because if you get too close, the gas whooshes out and you can get scorched! You acted like I was stupid or something and you used the paper match – and now look. You're bald…with a seared scalp. Or when I told you that you shouldn't go swimming right after you eat because you'd get cramps and you said, "that's an old wives' tale" and then you got cramps anyway and almost drowned. I keep trying to save you – and you won't let me! And so here we are, once again, and I'm telling you, "I'm a vampire" – and you won't listen! So if you care about us – you and me – then you need to be out of town when the full moon arrives. Because a vampire – excuse me, vampiress – isn't responsible for whom she bites.

ENDING 1

I mean, on the one hand – sure, it'd be nice if I bit you and turned you into a vampire, too. We could live together for all eternity, living off other people's blood and generally wreaking havoc. But you're such a nice guy, and I hate for you to end up like me. You ever try sleeping in a coffin? It's stuffy and uncomfortable and it sucks! So please, Richard, if you care about me, and you value your mortal life, get lost whenever there's a full moon. Okay?

ENDING 2

Well, now there's an idea, isn't it? If I bit you...and you turned into a vampire, too...why, we could both live forever! Oh, you'd love turning into a bat and flying to Transylvania with me for the winter! And we could live off the blood of others for a couple of hundred years and grow old together! We could have a coffin made for two and sleep side by side! What do you say, Richard? Are you feeling "batty?"

ENDING 3

_____
_____
_____
_____
_____
_____
_____
_____

MURDER FUSE

HE. I never, for a million years, would've dreamed that I could kill a man. Growing up like we did, in a world of, of privilege…wealth…of limitless opportunity…you naturally just tend to think that you're above things like murder. But you're not. Nobody is. I guess we all have this, this fuse inside us…okay, call it the "murder fuse"…and if that fuse gets blown…that's it. *(beat)* They're calling it a crime of passion. But I didn't feel passion. I didn't even feel angry. Truth is, I'd thought about it so long, that when I finally did it, it was all very mechanical. Like it wasn't even me pulling the trigger. Like I was watching a movie or something. You see, the hate had burned out of me long, long ago. All that was left was the desire…no, not even desire, that's too strong a word for what I was feeling…intent. This deep-seated intent to succeed. I knew I was going to kill him. I knew I *had* to. I knew with every fiber of my being that killing him was the only way I'd ever get justice. And from that moment on, some part of my brain was always working out the problem, no matter what else I was doing. I could be paying bills…doing the laundry…even standing there in the lecture hall, talking about isotopes, but deep inside, my brain was systematically trying to figure out, "Where could I corner him?" "Can I get him alone?" "How will I do it?" You know how your brain works things out when you're asleep? Like, unconscious activity? Well, this was much like that. Twenty-four hours a day, my brain was computing how I might kill Brian Daniels. And one night, as I was snoring away the hours…bingo. My brain figured it all out for me.

ENDING 1

(pause) In case you didn't notice, that was more or less a confession. I killed the cockroach. And I'd do it again. When somebody – when a guy like him – takes the most precious thing from you...in my case, my child... the fuse gets blown and you will do anything – *anything* – for revenge. You think you're different. You look at me like you can't even imagine what I'm saying. But I promise you, if you went through what I did...you'd have done the same.

ENDING 2

(pause) I'm not proud of it. It's just what happened. My brain was like a computer...information was fed into it...in this case, that he'd killed my daughter and nobody was going to do anything about it...and so the computer went to work, trying to process that information. The result was, that I had to go do what I did. Like I said, I'm not proud of it...but, for whatever reason, some fuse inside me got blown and I had to act.

ENDING 3

_____

_____

_____

_____

_____

_____

_____

_____

UNRULY BEHAVIOR

SHE. I can't *believe* you did that! In front of all my friends! Oh, don't act like you don't know what I'm talking about! You know full well what I'm talking about, Melville! You pulled your *pants* down! In the dining room! During the dessert course! *(beat)* I *know* you were wearing your underwear, that's not the point, it was still offensive! *(lowering her voice, as if those in the next room can hear:)* These are well-heeled, high-society types, they don't want to see your underwear! They don't want to see *anybody's* underwear! I doubt if they ever see their *own* underwear! And you knew that! I *know* you knew it, Melville, because I know you, and I know what you know and I know how you think and I know you thought that I would think this was offensive! What I don't get is why you chose do something like this here – now – knowing it would hurt me. Knowing it would embarrass me. Knowing that I would look like an idiot in the eyes of my friends. Yes, "friends," Melville, but of course, how would you know what a friend is anyway, you live with a three-legged pit bull and a boa constrictor and play with electric train sets all night long. A grown man, playing with plastic cabooses! Well, forgive me if I sound like a big sister, but I *am* your big sister and *you...*you're a big disappointment. *(beat)* There, I've said it. It's been swimming around in my head all these years, and I just...I don't *understand*, Melville. Back when we were kids, you were the one to beat! You had the looks, the grades, the attitude...everybody wanted to be like you! Especially me! *Most* of all, me! I was this nerdy, stupid wallflower with a mouthful of braces, but you...you were something else!

ENDING 1

(beat) What happened? You had everything going for you and it's like you just – just gave up. Adopted this weird, childish persona and just…surrendered. It's not funny, Melville. And it's not charming. It's upsetting, that's what it is. And if you want to continue to have a relationship with me, it needs to stop. Now. I want you to go back in there and apologize. I mean it! Pull your pants up and tell them all you're off your medication or – something. You can do it, Melville. I'm depending on you to make this right.

ENDING 2

You knew how much this party meant to me. I told you. I pounded it into your thick skull. Somehow I knew, deep inside myself, that you would pull some weird stunt. Something like this. But I guess I'm the eternal optimist. I kept hoping that you were better than that. Please be better than that, Melville. I want you to be better. I want you to be the kind of big brother I can look up to again. Can't you do that for me?

ENDING 3

_____

_____

_____

_____

_____

_____

_____

_____

MIXING UP THE MIX

HE. I've never been so insulted in all my life! What's the point of having your own country club if you can't exclude other people? I am a dues paying member! I demand that you keep Frederic Persiliovich off this property! Because! He's not a member! In order to be a member, he has to be nominated by an existing member and – what? What do you mean, I nominated him? I certainly did not! In fact, I've never nominated anybody! All these years, I've refused to nominate anyone because I don't want "The Mix" to change! Yes, you heard me right! I said, the Mix! Country Club membership is, at its core, and must be, elitist. A careful balance must be maintained. No boors, no bullies, no riff-raff. My great-grandfather took a stand when he founded this place and I am charged with maintaining the quality of it! Granted, I've lost several colleagues for taking that stand, but I took a stand, and what good is a stand if you don't reinforce it? And now you come in here and tell me that an ill-mannered Russian with too much cologne is – well, I don't care if he's not a Russian. He sounds like a Russian. He looks like a Russian. He smells like a Russian. For all intents and purposes, he should be a Russian. And that accent of his...it's positively old-world Soviet Bloc. He doesn't belong in here! My great grandfather built this place with his bare hands – well, he *hired* the people who built it – and I will not let you overrun it with the Russian Mafia! Why do you keep saying that? Why do you keep saying I nominated him? I didn't nominate him! I – *(stops)* What? By *written ballot?* Let me see... *(squints as if reading something)* That's *my* handwriting! Is this some kind of trick? Why would I nominate this man for *anything,* let alone a Country Club membership!?

ENDING 1

(offended:) I was *not* drunk! Well, at least not *that* drunk! I am a well-bred man, Folger. I know how to handle my port! There is no way I could've become so intoxicated with drink as to... *(suddenly remembers:)* Oh, dear. You may be right, Folger. There was that one night I... *(suddenly in crisis mode:)* Quick! Get the By-Laws! There must be *some* way to un-nominate a nominee!

ENDING 2

He...what? He'll tell the media that I...? Well, this is blackmail! I'm not going to admit someone of his low social order to this establishment simply because he thinks he can blackmail me with... *(pause)* Really? He knows everything? Well, then...I suppose there are circumstances when one must compromise. After all, one must protect oneself. All right, then. He's in.

ENDING 3

_____
_____
_____
_____
_____
_____
_____
_____

CONFEDERATE ARMY WIFE

SHE. Excuse me, Darlene. Let me just deal with the children right quick. *(yells off:)* William Ben Walter Junior! You come in here, right this instant! I mean it! No child of mine is going to sculpt his sister's hair with axle grease and get away with it! *(shuddering, to Darlene:)* Ooh, these boys! They are unmanageable! It's been this way ever since William Ben Walter Senior went off to war. Oh, not a *real* war. The re-enactment war. He serves under Bogg Henry Tatum, who plays General Robert E. Lee, in the Engagement at Cheat Mountain, Virginia. Well, it's West Virginia now, but it was Virginia in 1861... amazing how much you learn, bein' married to a Civil War Historian. Well, part-time historian, full-time gas station attendant. *(yells off:)* William Jefferson Walter, you let him go! You do not drag your brother around the house by his nose, do you hear me? It's liable to come off in your hand, and then what would we do? He'd look like *The Planet of the Apes*! *(to Darlene:)* It's so hard bein' a Confederate Army Wife. Billy don't like me comin' with him to the re-enactment. He says it's a "man thing" and that all the men leave their wives at home. I miss him so when he's off at war. It's like my own war here at home, just keepin' these little rug rats from killin' each other. *(yells off:)* Dishwashin' soap is *not* a food group, young man! Don't you dare! You – listen to me! Do *not* fill your little brother's bottle with that soap! I'm warning you! If you do, you will be the one changin' his diapers tonight! *(back to Darlene:)* I've been thinkin' about askin' Billy to lay out of next year's re-enactment. Kinda chews up my nerves when he's gone. Only thing is, it's hard to ask Billy to do things...he tends to get...well, angry.

ENDING 1

(fights back tears.) Do you ever wake up and think you married the wrong man, Darlene? I swear, I hate to have thoughts like that in my head, but there are days...days when I think, I should've married Henry Jackson. There he is, up in Hartford, Connecticut with a law firm and a great big house...but then again, I'd be a Yankee, wouldn't I? And we certainly couldn't have that*! (yells off:)* I swear to God, if you throw your brother through that window, I'm comin' in there!

ENDING 2

Momma says that I should just be a "good wife" and not ask for much. She says the roof over my head is more than I deserve. You know momma, she just ekes out her day watchin' game shows and drinkin' her liver away...I just sometimes wonder...if there's more to life. More than wrestlin' these boys into their clothes and waitin' for Billy. Oh, but listen to me. Runnin' off at the mouth like that. I'm just not very good when he's off at war...even a pretend one!

ENDING 3

_____

_____

_____

_____

_____

_____

_____

_____

BOBBING FOR DENTURES

HE. I ain't seen your false teeth, papaw. I don't know where they could be. Did you leave 'em on the bus again? Man, that one time you left 'em on the bus and I had to sweet-talk that big, fat, smelly ol' bus driver lady into diggin' 'em out from under the back seat and givin' 'em to me. *(shudders at the memory)* I'll tell ya right now, I ain't doin' that again. *(an idea:)* Oh! Maybe they're floatin' in the toilet bowl, like that one time. I made you reach in there after 'em, though, 'member? There wasn't no way I was gonna go bobbin' for dentures! I mean, I have done a good many disgusting things in my time but I draw the line outta fishin' in the bowl for your teeth! Papaw, you got to learn to keep up with 'em! Makes us look like trailer trash, with a papaw that's stumblin' around who ain't got no teeth in his head. I am a respectable young man. I go out there, lookin' for work, and I got a reputation to uphold. Don't laugh at me, I'm serious. You got to help me create a reputation for myself. *(scoffs:)* No, reputation is not a six-dollar word. It's more like a two-dollar word. I learned it in school. Well, I'm sorry you think it's funny, me goin' to night school, but I don't wanna wind up livin' in a trailer park, fishin' my teeth out of the toilet. I wanna wind up in a nice house out in Moose Run. *(beat)* Moose Run. It's that new subdivision out on Creek Bed Drive. I know you don't want to live there – don't worry! You'll go to your grave in this doublewide, I'm sure of if. Probably drown, fishing your teeth out of the bowl. Just…put 'em back in, will you? And button up your shirt. You got to think about how you look once in awhile, papaw. Have some respect for yourself. That's your main trouble, you know. You ain't never had no respect for yourself.

ENDING 1

Now, look. Everybody else done moved away. I'm the only one left here to look after you. If you want lookin' after, then you gotta play by my rules. Understand? I don't mind helpin' you get your groceries and pay your bills and clean up the place, but you gotta help me out by showin' some kind of appreciation. Bein' stubborn ain't gonna help you win this fight, papaw. Working with me will. Now what's it gonna be?

ENDING 2

All right. I've said it. I've said everything I can, and nothin' gets through that thick head o' yours. You just laugh and shake your head and...well, I'm telling you! I'm though. You done run everybody off but me and you know what? I've taken as much as I can out of you. I'm through. From now on, you can find your own teeth. I'm gonna make somethin' out of my life, papaw. I ain't windin' up like you!

ENDING 3

_____
_____
_____
_____
_____
_____
_____
_____

THE RED LIST

SHE. I understand what you're saying. I used to be a miserable person, too, Connie. Depressed...angry... resentful...but one day, I turned a corner! I changed. Without medication, too! And now, I'm happy, pleasant and fulfilled, all the time. Day or night, you'll always find me smiling. What's my secret, you ask? It's simple: I punish other people. Seriously. From the endless list of individuals that I can't stand or won't tolerate or despise...or simply *hate*...I pick one person each day and cause something bad to happen to them. Whether it's tripping that simple old man who shuffles past the outdoor café every afternoon...or sneaking onto Archibald's computer and logging onto inappropriate websites...striking back gives me deep and lasting satisfaction! It raises my spirits! It makes me whole again! I know Archibald got fired. I didn't say there weren't consequences. But that made me happy, too! I was practically giddy that day! *(laughs, then sighs)* I wish you'd try it. You see, I can tell you all this because *you're* not on my Red List. That's the list of people I can't stand. You're on the Blue List – which is rather brief, I'll admit – but that means you're safe from my revenge! I like you! *(laughs)* Well, unless you do something to piss me off, and I know you won't do that, will you, Connie? You're such a pal! And...speaking of being a pal, I need you to do an eensy-weensie little favor for me...you know that new manager who started on Friday? Carlos. Yes, well, he insulted me when he arrived. He said it was so nice to meet someone here "his own age." Well, I'm ten years younger than him – at least. Not a good way to start a working relationship, I'm afraid. It made me sad. Very sad. So I need you to help me out a little bit...I want you to get the key to his office. Yes. Carlos' office.

ENDING 1

Why? Because some very humiliating phone calls are going to be made from his phone! To whom? Well that's for me to know and you to wonder about, isn't it? Now don't say "no," Connie. I've never asked you for anything before, and I'd hate for you to wind up on my Red List...wouldn't you? I promise you, that's not where you want to be. So what do you say, Connie? The key? We're the only two will ever know about it!

ENDING 2

Why? Because some very humiliating phone calls are going to be made from his phone! To who? Well that's for me to know and you to wonder about, isn't it? Connie! Don't over-react! I was just asking...yes, I realize what I'm saying, but it's not like you don't have a choice! You owe me! I've kept you on the Blue List all this time and after all, you want to stay there, don't you? Don't you? Connie? Connie! Where are you going? Connie!

ENDING 3

_____

_____

_____

_____

_____

_____

_____

_____

THE MASK

HE. People can change, Serena. People can definitely change. I know it for a fact. A few years ago, I got to a point in my life when I was absolutely consumed by hate. A deep, blinding hatred of everyone and everything around me. I woke up full of hate and went to bed full of hate. It dominated every waking thought and filled every sleeping dream. My only real motive, as I went about my daily walk and conversation, was to try and find some way to lash out and harm someone else. I know, it sounds surprising now...you've never seen that side of me, have you? But it was there, all right. That's why I speak from experience when I say that a person can change. In my case, it was a lot of prayer and a lot of self-searching. I realized that I didn't have to live that way...that there was a greater power than me, out there, that could govern my thoughts and actions. And that, if I found some way to let go...and not hang onto all the dark feelings I was harboring... that a profound change could take place inside me. I'm not trying to get all mumbo-jumbo on you, but I did have an epiphany. It hit me like a bolt of lighting... and it was so clear. I'd been wearing a mask. All I had to do was take it off – and let it go. It wasn't so much me that changed, exactly...but I realized that the hateful person, that bastard I'd become, wasn't who I really *was*...who I really was – *am* – is good. Decent. Caring. I can see that in you, too, Serena. I know you can't, but trust me, it's there. Take it from someone who knows. You want to change, and you think it's impossible... but it's not something you have to do. Who you want to be...is who you already are.

ENDING 1

Serena – Ser – well, don't throw it back in my face! All I'm doing is trying to *help*! You came to me and said you were miserable! Well, I'm just saying...I went through what I think you're going through and I came out the other side. There *is* another side, Serena. And if you'd just quit being so stubborn, so iron-willed... you could find it. It's as easy as waking up. So for God's sake, wake up!

ENDING 2

No, it's not a bunch of new-age crap. It's true! You say you want to be loving and kind towards your family instead of mean and hateful. Okay; well, then do it! *(beat)* I see. Well, it's your choice. If you want to be that way, that's your prerogative. But for God's sake, Serena. There is another way.

ENDING 3

_____

_____

_____

_____

_____

_____

_____

_____

NICED TO DEATH

SHE. I've figured out the ultimate weapon…the best way to defeat all my enemies. I *nice* 'em to death! That's right. And you wouldn't *believe* their reaction – it stops 'em dead in their tracks! Really and truly, when somebody's being nice to them, they don't know *what* to do! You see, usually, when people raise their voices and start to pick a fight…they *want* you to get all riled-up and fight back. And when they start screaming at you it's because they want *you* to start screaming back at them! But I don't do that anymore. I just smile. I'm quiet. I'm nice. I lower my voice… *(She does, and whispers:)* …and it totally *blows their minds. (for example:)* The other day, my boss came stomping over to my cubicle – I could hear him three aisles away – and he SCREAMED – so loud that practically everybody on the third floor could hear him – "What were you *thinking*, sending out a letter like this out to a client!? Are you stupid?" Now, naturally, he wanted me to start yelling back, something like, "No, I'm not stupid, *you're* stupid!" But instead, I just…smiled. *(She does.)* And I said, so softly he could barely hear me, "I'm so sorry you didn't like it, Mr. Beasley." And at first he didn't know what was happening. He just started stammering and sputtering, "What? What?" And I kept right on smiling. I didn't allow my rage to bubble up. It was down there, all right, like the inside of a volcano, but I just smiled…and said…"Would you like a cold glass of water?" Well, I thought he was going to *faint*! He turned the strangest shade of purple and walked away. And two hours later…he *apologized*! So I've just been being nice to each and every person I meet!

ENDING 1

You might try it sometimes, Elroy. You tend to be a disagreeable sort. *(reacts:)* I'm not trying to upset you! I'm telling you for your own good! You tend to get...well...prickly, sometimes. I would think you'd get much farther along in life if you were nice instead. How long has it been since you even smiled? Hmm? C'mon, now...see if those lips can even make a smile...there! Isn't that better?!

ENDING 2

Well, you don't have to go getting all *livid* at me, Elroy! You'd think I just called your mother a bad name or something! All I was trying to do was share the benefit of my experience with you, and the least you could do is...what? *(shocked:)* Well, SAME TO YOU, BUSTER! *(then, reacting with great pleasure:)* OOOOH, that felt GOOD! Ooooh, I've been stuffing all this anger inside of me for WEEKS now, but thanks to you, I'M GONNA LET IT ALLLLL OUT – AT YOU! *(furious:)* ARE YOU *HAPPY, ELROY*!?!

ENDING 3

_____
_____
_____
_____
_____
_____
_____
_____

APPENDIX –
GUIDELINES FOR WRITING ENDINGS

First of all, make sure that you are *talking to someone specific*. It doesn't matter who it is (there are no right or wrong choices in writing monologues, but there must be choices). It might be your best friend, your parents, a blind date, a group of people – or simply an imaginary person you create for this exercise. The most important thing is to make the relationship very specific in your own mind, so that, as you begin to write, you will know from the start how the other person (or people) might react to what you're saying. How they react will directly affect what you write.

Establish specifically *where this conversation is taking place*. If it's in your home, and you're alone with the other person, the content will be different than if you were in a crowded restaurant.

Make sure you are *pursuing an objective* – trying to get something – that you really want, and could reasonably get, from the other person. This doesn't have to be a *thing*; maybe you're trying to get the other person to agree with you, or to say something specific in response – or perhaps you're asking them to do something for you. You could be seeking their approval. But you must want something specific from the other person. You don't have to come right out and ask for it literally during the monologue, but you do have to try to achieve your objective.

Try to create an obstacle – in other words, a reason the person you're speaking to might not want to give you what you want. This requires you to put yourself in the other character's head. If what you're trying to get is something which the other person would happily give to you or do for you, there's no sense of conflict, no drama. Ideally, you've got to push to get whatever it is you want from the other person – that is what will make your monologue come alive.

You may have to change tactics to get what you're after – depending on how the imaginary person you're talking to is reacting (or *not* reacting, as the case may be) to what you're saying. For example, if halfway through the speech the person to whom you're speaking gets mad at you and tells you to "shut up," then what you're saying isn't working and you'll have to try a different approach – perhaps something quieter, kinder, gentler. A change of tactics provides a great showcase for the actor because it allows you to display other facets of yourself in your audition speech.

TO RECAP:

ESTABLISH *SPECIFICALLY* WHO YOU'RE TALKING TO

ESTABLISH *SPECIFICALLY* WHERE THE CONVERSATION IS
TAKING PLACE

ESTABLISH *SPECIFICALLY* WHAT YOUR OBJECTIVE IS

ESTABLISH THE OBSTACLE(S) TO ACHIEVING YOUR OBJECTIVE

IF NECESSARY, CHANGE TACTICS DURING THE MONOLOGUE

...AND HAVE FUN!!!

Also by
Jason Milligan...

...And the Rain Came to Mayfield
5 Easy Pieces
Any Friend of Percy D'Angelino is a Friend of Mine
The Best Warm Beer in Brooklyn
Both Sides of the Story
Can't Buy Me Love
Clara and the Gambler
Class of '77
Cross Country
Exodus From McDonaldland
Family Values
The Fire-Breaathing Lady and the Sugarplum Fairy
The Genuine Article
Getting Even
Going Solo
His & Hers
Instincts
John's Ring
Juris Prudence
Key Lime Pie
Less Said, the Better
Life After Elvis
Lullaby
Men in Suits
Money Talks
New York Stories: Five Plays About Life in New York
Next Tuesday
Next!
Nights in Hohokus
One Way Street
Paul's Ghost
The Prettiest Girl in Lafayette County
The Quality of Boiled Water
Rituals
Rivals
Road Trip
Shoes
Shore Leave
Spit in Yazoo City
Strange as It May Seem...
Waiting for Ringo
Walking on the Moon
Willy Wallace Chats... With the Kids

Please visit our website **samuelfrench.com** for complete
descriptions and licensing information.

NOW AVAILABLE FROM SAMUEL FRENCH!

EXCEPTIONAL MONOLOGUES FOR MEN & WOMEN

Volume One

Edited by Roxane Heinze-Bradshaw and
Katherine DiSavino

In an effort to foster awareness of new plays, and provide for the ever-constant need of audition material, we are proud to announce a new series of monologue books highlighting the latest Samuel French publications. Each year, starting with 2008, monologues from or most recent publications will be selected by our editorial staff to be included in that year's collection. Complete with play synopses, a thematic index, and broad range of styles, you are sure to find one that suits your audition needs. A wonderful way to sample our latest publications, too! Volume 1 includes such titles and authors as: *Eurydice* by Sarah Ruhl, *The Receptionist* by Adam Bock, *In the Continuum* by Danai Gurira & Nikkole Salter, *Bach at Leipzig* by Itamar Moses, and many more.

CPSIA information can be obtained at www.ICGtesting.com
Printed in the USA
LVOW081504270911

248099LV00001B/58/P